WORK AND WAGES

LONDON: PRINTED BY
SPOTTISWOODE AND CO., NEW-STREET SQUARE
AND PARLIAMENT STREET

WORK AND WAGES

PRACTICALLY ILLUSTRATED

BY

THOMAS BRASSEY, M. P.

NEW YORK:
D. APPLETON AND COMPANY,
549 & 551 BROADWAY.
1872.

THIS WORK IS DEDICATED

By Permission

TO

THOMAS HUGHES, Q.C., M.P.

AS A MARK OF APPRECIATION OF

HIS EMINENT SERVICES IN MEDIATING BETWEEN THE

EMPLOYERS AND THE EMPLOYED

PREFACE.

As I have been in some measure the cause of this work being produced, and have seen it through the press, it may be desirable for me to give some account of its origin and its purpose.

While I was writing the Life of the late Mr. Brassey, the Labour question was naturally much in my thoughts; and I could not but observe that, in studying his Life, many facts of high importance in relation to the general state of labour throughout the world came prominently forward.

I found that my coadjutor, Mr. Thomas Brassey, was fully aware of the value of these facts, and had already given great attention to the question of labour in all its various aspects. I asked him, therefore, to give me a paper on the subject, dealing especially with Wages, and taking his illustrations from the facts which were known to us both from the evidence that had been given by many skilled persons in reference to his father's career. This paper I proposed to subjoin to the Life.

It was soon found, however, that though the experience which the late Mr. Brassey had gained, as regards the labour question, was perhaps as large and varied as had ever fallen to the lot of any one man to acquire for himself, it still occupied only one branch of the subject. To treat this subject with the fulness that it inevitably demands, a general survey of the labour employed in all trades and occupations was needed. Mr. Thomas Brassey's unremitting industry, based upon much previous research, has supplied evidence of the most varied and extensive kind;

and now, the facts which were originally gained from the study of his father's experience, form but a small part of the work, when compared with those which have been elicited by studying the other branches of industry that have been carefully examined. As regards some special departments of labour, there have been more exhaustive researches; but such a body of evidence, so comprehensive and so various, bearing upon the whole subject of labour generally, and not even favouring any particular section of it, has never, I think, been brought together in the comparatively small compass of a single volume.

Mr. Thomas Brassey would not for a moment contend that several of the conclusions he has arrived at, are new to students of Political Economy. The aspects, however, of these conclusions, and the practical effect which should be given to them, vary much according to the circumstances of the times, a fact which the author has not lost sight of.

It is, however, very satisfactory to find that the most recent facts are entirely in accord with some of the chief principles laid down by Adam Smith and the earlier masters of political economy.

It has been to me, and I doubt not that it will be to many of the readers of this book, a very pleasing thing to find that the author is able, by an overwhelming mass of evidence, to dispel the fear which has long prevailed of our industrial labours being about to be greatly restricted by foreign competition, based upon the comparative cheapness of wages in foreign countries.

Mr. Brassey's remarks in reference to the action of Trades Unions, appear to me, to be at the present moment, of the highest importance, and to indicate thoroughly sound and just views of the duties and responsibilities, both of employers and employed.

ARTHUR HELPS.

LONDON: June 1872.

CONTENTS.

INTRODUCTION.

IT has been suggested that the publication of a memoir of my father affords a seasonable opportunity for collating the results of his long and varied experience of the cost of labour, and also of setting forth results of a kindred character. Other men have organized and conducted vast industrial operations; but few have laboured in so many lands, or had the same means of comparing the working men of every nation.

INTRODUCTION.

The task of writing the following pages has been a serious addition to the engrossing labours of Parliamentary life. But I can truly say that it has been to me a labour of

INTRODUCTION.

love, for which I shall be well rewarded if the facts which are here recorded prove a useful addition to the store of knowledge on this important subject, and valuable to economists, whose study of the science of wages and whose able writings have contributed so much to enlighten even practical men.

The altered conditions of modern industry seem likely to lead to new complications in the relations between labour and capital. Close competition with the cheaper labour of other countries makes it necessary for our manufacturers to develop to the utmost the use of machinery, and this can be best effected in large establishments.

Class jealousies between employers and employed.

Between the employer and the employed there is now a wider interval than before; and with the diminished opportunities of personal intercourse, there is a danger that class prejudices and class jealousies may be embittered.

If ignorance be, as undoubtedly it is, the origin of every prejudice, let us rest assured that clearer knowledge will bring charity and forbearance, where jealousy and distrust now unhappily divide the master and the man. It was well said by Le Père Hyacinthe, "Toutes les fois que le voisin commet une faute, accusons-nous nous-mêmes, nous ne l'avons pas assez édifié."

There have been many high examples of generosity and consideration for the working men among the great employers of England. I desire to follow humbly in their footsteps, and I ask that the spirit of impartiality on labour questions which may perhaps be recognised throughout this essay, may be accepted as an earnest of my good intentions.

Few persons are more indebted to the labourers and artisans of this country than I am; and I shall ever be found ready to sympathise with their difficulties and to vindicate their rights. While I feel myself impelled, by many and potent influences, to take the employers' view of the labour question, on the other hand I cannot forget that the working classes, of whom vast numbers for many years rendered honest and faithful services to my father, possess especial claims on my sympathy and gratitude.

England's glory.

I know that there are some who fear that the day of England's commercial glory is departed. I can see no reason for sharing in those alarms.

> O passi graviora! dabit Deus his quoque finem.

I have a high opinion of the industry and common sense of our working people, and I look forward with unshaken confidence to the continued prosperity of my country.

WORK AND WAGES

PRACTICALLY ILLUSTRATED.

CHAPTER I.

HISTORICAL SKETCH—STRIKES—TRADES UNIONS.

CHAP. I.

Recognition of the rights of labour.

THE recognition of the rights of free labour came late in the history of the world. Neither the Greeks nor the Romans recognised the liberty of labour.

From the third to the thirteenth century the Church was the most faithful protector of the labouring man. From the thirteenth to the eighteenth century, as we have been told by M. Michael Chevalier, from whose writings these historical details are borrowed,

CHAP. I.

the Parliaments, the Legists, and the Lawyers, did much to secure liberty for the labourer.

Turgot on the rights of labour.

Turgot, the First Minister of Louis XVI., fully appreciated the rights of free labour. In his Edict of 1776 he says:—"Dieu, en donnant à l'homme des besoins, a fait du droit de travailler la propriété de tous les hommes, et cette propriété est la première, la plus sacrée, et la plus imprescriptible de toutes."

This Edict, the first proclamation of the just and equitable principles which are now universally accepted, was cancelled in the darker times, after the fall of Turgot.

Public opinion.

The right of free labour has, however, at length been fully recognised by a power which far transcends that of Parliaments or Kings, I mean the power of public opinion. Consequently the right of combination, for the purpose of obtaining better terms for labour, has now been conceded to the working men of every country in Europe, which has reached a high degree of civilization. And here I would point out, that the tendency to combination for the purpose of promoting their

CHAP. I.

mutual interests is no new thing among the industrial classes. The Guilds of the Middle Ages were but the forerunners of the Trades Unions of to-day, and the "Strikes" of modern times have had their counterpart in the Jacquerie riots of the fourteenth century.

Trade Guilds.

When we take into view the great changes which have been brought about in the industrial organization of this country during the present century—the substitution of steam for manual power, and of machinery for hand labour, and remember that the resources of machinery can be most fully developed only when applied on a large scale, the reasons why workmen have gathered together in recent times, in numbers so vast, round our great industrial centres, are not far to seek.

Origin of Trades Unions.

When operatives have thus been assembled together in great numbers, under the same roof, tending the same machine, and working at the same table, is it not natural—nay reasonable—that they should confer and take action together on all questions of mutual interest? In this most legitimate manner Trades Unions have had their origin.

CHAP. I.

Faults of Trades Unions.

I am not insensible to the great errors and follies which have marked the policy and the conduct of certain Trades Unions. In regard to wages, as distinguished from "benefit objects," their influence has too often been essentially illiberal, anti-social, and calculated to establish, among the industrial classes of this country, that subdivision of caste which has been the great curse of India.

There is a general tendency amongst the Trades Unions to ignore the interest of the master, as if his success were not essential to their own prosperity. In his evidence before the Trades Unions Commissioners, Mr. Connolly, of the Masons' Society, made a frank confession that their rules were for the men, not the masters. "They want," he said, "the greatest profit, we the highest wages."

Trades Unions cannot regulate wages.

I am not afraid of the Trades Unions. On the contrary, I believe that their power, both for good and for evil, has been greatly exaggerated. When the demand for labour is increasing, the employers compete against each other for the supply of labour, and wages will necessarily rise.

CHAP. I.

Evidence of Mr. Mault.

The pretensions of the Trades Unions to regulate the rate of wages, irrespectively of the demand for labour, are wholly at variance with the most prominent facts. Mr. Mault, the secretary to the Builders' Association of Birmingham, stated to the Trades Unions Commissioners, that, of the 900,000 men employed in the building trades, not more than 90,000 were members of Trades Unions; and that, although the Trades Unions professed to aim at securing uniformity of wage throughout the country, the wages of masons varied in different parts from $4\frac{1}{2}$*d.* to $7\frac{3}{8}$*d.* per hour, the wages of bricklayers from $4\frac{1}{2}$*d.* to 8*d.*, and those of carpenters from $4\frac{5}{8}$*d.* to $8\frac{1}{2}$*d.* These figures conclusively prove the fallacy of the idea that Trades Unions can secure for their clients an uniform rate of wages.

Uniform wages.

Trades Unions may secure an earlier advance.

Their organization and united action may secure an advance of wages at a somewhat earlier date; but, eventually the competition among employers would be equally beneficial to the working people. The advantage to the working classes of obtaining an advance

CHAP. I.

at an earlier date is not, in my opinion, sufficient to compensate for the expense of perpetually maintaining, by heavy subscriptions, the Trades Union organization, still less to compensate for the loss which is caused by unsuccessful strikes.

Strikes against a falling market always fail.

I have admitted that Trades Unions may have the effect of obtaining an advance in wages at an earlier date; but the most protracted strikes, in which the working men have been engaged have generally taken place, not for the purpose of securing an advance in wages, but for the purpose of resisting a fall. Resistance to a proposed reduction was the cause of the engineers' strike in 1852; of the strike at Preston in 1853; of the strike in the iron trade in 1865; and of the strike of the colliers at Wigan in 1868. In each of these cases the masters had found it necessary, in consequence of the depressed state of trade, to reduce the rate of wages; but the men, ignoring the circumstances of the trade, and looking only to what they believed to be a degradation of their position as workmen, refused to accept the reduction.

They therefore went out on strike; but, after a protracted struggle, were compelled to accept the original proposal of their employers.

Uniform wages.

It has been a great object with Trades Unions to establish uniformity of wage, irrespective of the personal abilities of the workman. The effect of this system is obviously unjust to the more skilful and capable artisan, while, at the same time, experience shows that the inferior artisan does not by any means escape the ill effects of such a system. Perhaps in the long run, he it is who suffers most. Mr. Smith, in his evidence before the Trades Unions Commissioners, said, "I have always been against a uniform rate of wage. The moment there is a reduction in the shops or works, all the men who, from age or other causes, cannot do their full share, are discharged, although they might be employed continuously at lower wages."

Employers dislike to reduce wages.

Employers, as a general rule, from motives of kindness and consideration towards their workmen, are anxious to avoid, if they possibly can, reductions of wages. They rarely

CHAP. I.

ask their workpeople to accept a lower rate of wages, until the condition of their trade has become so unfavourable, as to make the reduction absolutely necessary.

This opinion is confirmed by Mr. John Stuart Mill, who says that "Wages, like other things, are regulated, either by competition or by custom. In this country there are few kinds of labour, of which the remuneration would not be lower than it is, if the employers took the full advantage of competition." The success which marked Mr. Brassey's career has become matter of notoriety; but no employer ever dealt more liberally with labour. The almost invariable result of the commencement of railway operations in any county in England, or in any country abroad, was a rise in the prevalent rate of wages. On one occasion an estimate was submitted to him for a contract, for which a sharp competition was expected. The prices had accordingly been cut down to an unusually low figure. He thereupon asked "How it was proposed to carry out the work for such inadequate prices?" In reply, it was stated that the calculation was based on the assumption that a reduction of wages could be negotiated. On receiving this explanation he desisted from all further examination of the estimate, saying, that "If business could only be obtained by screwing down wages, he would rather be without it." A similar feeling I believe to be generally entertained by employers.

Power of the masters in combination.

The power of combination has been proved, by experience of its results, to be at least as much for the advantage of the masters as the workmen. The defeat of the shipwrights on the Thames in 1852, and more recently the failure of the iron workers' strike in Staffordshire, are conspicuous examples of the power which the masters acquire by combination among themselves.

Exaggerated pretensions of certain agitators during strikes.

The great evil, however, of Trades Unions, in their action in regard to the wage question, arises from the fact that the leaders of these societies, while they exercise great authority over the members of the Trades Unions, have no corresponding power of obtaining for their clients what they tell them they

CHAP. I.

ought to have. No virtue is so freely displayed as the virtue of generosity, when exercised in imagination at the expense of others. Trades Union agitators have too often sought to win the admiration of their auditory by thoughtless declamation against the alleged rapacity of employers, and by loud professions of sympathy with the wrongs of their industrial brethren. Their credulous hearers have been apt to forget that, when the trade in which they are employed is yielding no profit, or is perhaps being carried on at a loss, it is better for the employer to abandon, for the time, a business in which he has hitherto persevered only in the hope of an ultimate revival of trade, rather than consent to give rates of pay which must inevitably involve him in disaster.

Ignorance of the trade shown by leaders of strikes.

The leaders in several protracted strikes have exhibited a melancholy ignorance of the state of their own trade, and even of the market value of the goods, in the production of which they are engaged. How much suffering might have been spared to the working classes, if they had but known, before they engaged in a hopeless struggle,

The strike at Wigan.

the true merits of their case! I was once present at a meeting of employers during a large strike in the coal trade. I had the means of knowing that the wages which had been offered were the highest which the employers could afford to pay, and that the markets were so overstocked that it was a positive advantage to suspend the working of the pits for a time. But the facts which I had the means of knowing were apparently unknown to the miners; and it was indeed lamentable to see the hard-earned accumulations of many years exhausted in an obstinate resistance to a reduction of wage, which had not been proposed by the employers until it had been forced upon them by the unfavourable condition of their trade.

Power of oratory over ignorance.

The power of oratory over illiterate persons is irresistible. Some years ago, when the Birkenhead Docks were being constructed, a strike occurred among the labourers, most of whom were Irish, and such violence was displayed that a detachment of the 24th Regiment was sent to Birkenhead, to prevent a breach of the peace. The authors of this excitement among the workmen were three stump orators, who led out on strike the entire body of workmen employed, not less than 500 in number, not one of whom cared to enquire what justification there was for the demand which he had made upon his employers.

Conditions to be considered in striking.

The propriety of asking for an advance, and of striking if it is refused, depends entirely upon the state of trade, the amount of business in prospect, and the profits which the employers are enabled to realize, circumstances of which Trades Union agitators are too often wholly ignorant.

Moderation and sagacity of the superior officers of the stronger Unions.

But while I have thought it my duty to condemn the unreasonable proceedings of ignorant agitators, on the other hand I rejoice in the conviction that some of the most trusted leaders of the Trades Unions have profited by past experience, and are strongly averse to strikes. Mr. Allen, of the Amalgamated Engineers, stated to the Trades Unions Commissioners, that their Executive Council was always opposed to strikes. He added that their large accumulations, amounting to

149,000*l.*, only made the members of his society so much the more anxious not to waste their money in injudicious contests with their employers.

Trades Unions must watch the course of trade.

The first duty of the officers of the Trades Unions is, to understand the condition of their several trades, the demand for work, and the prices obtained. If these essential conditions of the wages problem were thoroughly understood by the workmen, many strikes would be prevented which cause inconvenience to employers, and bring consequences far more disastrous upon the workmen themselves.

We have a more abundant supply of materials than manufacturers on the Continent; but the cost of labour is greater in England.

Doubtless the dearness of labour in England has stimulated inventive genius and administrative skill; and, in fairness, the continued success of our trade should be attributed not only to the energy of the British workmen, but to improvement in the processes of manufacture, the merit of which is really due to the employers of labour. We have also had immense advantages in the comparative cheapness of fuel, and the abundant supply of iron and other raw materials of industry in England.

Mr. Lothian Bell.

"Here we raise 100,000,000 tons of coal per year, of which 10,000,000 tons are exported, and 20,000,000 are used in the iron works. In France and Belgium less than one fourth of this quantity is obtained, and that by great exertions."

Trades Unions should carefully watch the Continental labour market.

But it is not the less essential to keep a watchful eye on all that is taking place abroad. The organization of Trades Unions might be utilised for this important purpose. The resources of a joint purse should afford the means of sending delegates abroad, for whom opportunities ought to be provided of studying foreign languages, and whose duty it should be to keep the artisans of England closely informed of the fluctuations in the activity of trade and the reward of labour in the countries in which they resided. Trades Unions cannot in the long run materially influence the rate of wages, but there are many valuable services which they can render; and none would be more practically useful than the frequent publication of faithful reports on the state of the labour market from well placed observers on the Continent.

English workmen but imperfectly realize the serious odds against which our industrial establishments have to contend, from the difference in the rate of wages in this country and on the Continent. It requires much skill in the employer, much energy in the workmen, to compensate for the difference in wages.

Wages at Essen.

Perhaps the most successful engineering establishment on the Continent is M. Krupp's at Essen. Between 8,000 and 10,000 men are employed. Day workmen and helpers receive only 1*s.* 2½*d.* to 1*s.* 9½*d.* a day, while the wages of smiths, puddlers, carpenters, and masons, average 2*l.* 8*s.* to 6*l.* 15*s.* a month. These wages would not satisfy the English artisan; yet they are the highest which are paid in any part of Germany. This low rate of wages is to be explained partly by the cheapness of provisions; and it may here be remarked that the comparative cheapness of provisions in some districts of the Continent goes a long way to compensate our foreign

CHAP. I.

competitors for the higher price which they have to pay for coal and iron.

Moreover, the mode of living adopted by the artisans in Germany is more frugal than English habits will permit. A well informed writer in the 'Revue des Deux Mondes' states that at Essen 1,500 of the workmen live together in a barrack, where they have an eating room in common. In this barrack the workmen can procure food and lodging for the small sum of 10*d.* a day. The reviewer mentions that the favourite beverage of the workmen at Essen is coffee, and suggests that their preference for a cup, 'which cheers but not inebriates,' to intoxicating liquors, is worthy of imitation in other countries.

Excessive drinking.

It is creditable to the leaders of the Trades Societies that they have strenuously exerted their influence to suppress the vice of drunkenness. In spite of the development of industry in this country, the constantly increasing employment, and gradual increase in the rate of wages, we have to deplore the existence, side by side with this prosperity, of that which we are too apt to think is inevitable pauperism. Do not the statistics of the consumption of intoxicating liquors, and the expenditure of 100,000,000*l.* a year on drink, indicate an excessive indulgence in the use of stimulants? The taste for drinking which unhappily still prevails in this country among a large number of the labouring people has been excused on the ground that hard work renders a considerable consumption of beer almost a necessity. But some of the most powerful among the navvies have been teetotallers. On the Great Northern Railway there was a celebrated gang of navvies, who did more work in a day than any other gang on the line, and always left off work an hour or an hour and a half earlier than any other men. Every navvy in this powerful gang was a teetotaller.

The most powerful navvies teetotallers.

The working classes in the agricultural districts in France are, as a rule, much more provident than the same class in England. When the works were first commenced on the Paris and Rouen Railway, the contractors endeavoured to introduce a system by which the workmen were to be paid once a fortnight,

The French more provident than the English.

CHAP. I.

instead of once a week, as had been the custom in England. But very soon after operations had been begun, the Frenchmen requested that the pay might take place only once a month.

Paris and Rouen Railway.

Mr. Reid, managing director of the Paris and Rouen Railway, told the House of Commons Committee on Railway Labourers, in 1846, that a French labourer is a much more independent person than an Englishman, and much more respectable. He asserted in support of his opinion, this remarkable circumstance, that, whereas the French labourer desired to be paid only once a month, the English navvy desired to be paid on Saturday night—and, by the following Wednesday, he wanted something on account of the week's work. "Nothing could be a greater test," said Mr. Reid, "of the respectability of a working man, than being able to go without his pay for a month."

Rise in prices abroad.

In consequence of the additional activity of industry abroad, and the equalising effects of Free Trade on prices, enquiries in Spain, France, Belgium, and Prussia, show that provisions in those countries are from twenty to thirty per cent. dearer than twenty years ago. At the present time the prices of rent and clothing are about the same abroad as in England; but fuel is given to our workmen in the iron making districts at half the price charged to the workmen abroad. But, notwithstanding all these advantages, labour is about thirty per cent. cheaper, measured, that is to say, by the daily rate of wages on the Continent, than in this country. It is the opinion of Mr. Lothian Bell, one of our highest authorities, that, after all the efforts of our iron masters to contend with the difficulty of high-priced labour by the improvement of machinery, labour costs fifteen per cent. more in England than on the Continent, and this disadvantage in his opinion entirely neutralizes the advantages we derive from our great facilities in the proximity of our iron-mines to our coal-beds. Our workmen are not sufficiently alive to the necessity for the exercise of the utmost efforts of ingenuity, in order to enable capital invested

Labour cheaper abroad.

in England to hold its own in the industrial campaign.

Profits.

There is a notion that profits are higher in England than elsewhere. The large fortunes occasionally amassed in British industry are quoted in support of this assumption; but the different employments of stock are, as Adam Smith has observed, "more nearly on an equality than the necessary wages of the different sorts of labour. It seldom happens that great fortunes are made by any one regularly established and well-known branch of business, but in consequence of a long life of industry, frugality, and attention." These rare accumulations of wealth are generally the result of exceptional thrift, rather than exceptional gain. The low rate of interest which capital usually commands in England, as compared with foreign countries, is a conclusive proof that the profits of our trade are moderate.

In many continental markets we no longer enjoy the advantages which we formerly possessed; and foreign manufacturers, with their cheaper labour and more intimate knowledge of the character and requirements of the people, are rapidly gaining ground. Mr. Michell, in a letter on the condition of British trade in Russia, observes "that the Continent is getting an increasing proportion of the orders for rolling stock, tools, hardware, and metallic manufactures generally, except perhaps rails.

"English iron masters compete with difficulty with the works at Cologne, which supply many of the Russian railways with bridges. In the matter of tires English manufacturers have to a great extent been driven out of the market by Krupp.

"Of the large quantity of files now used in Russia, two-thirds come from Germany. Houses there purchase steel at Sheffield, and have it worked up into files in Prussia. English saws, on the contrary, meet with an increasing sale, their price having been reduced by one-half within the last few years.

"Zimmerman of Kilmitz supplies the Russian market with an enormous quantity of tools. He boasts of making Whitworth his model, and produces tools almost equally good

CHAP. I.

Imitations of English lathes are made in Germany for half the price, and largely imported into Russia.

Our trade with Russia affected by apprehension of strikes.

"Apart from the greater cheapness of continental hardware, dealers in Russia are frequently prevented from giving orders to English manufacturers by rumours of strikes. When these are reported, the dealers, not understanding that the disturbances are merely local, get alarmed at the possibility of their orders not being executed in time, and hence they prefer giving their orders in countries less liable to such serious contingencies.

"But there are other circumstances which should in fairness be mentioned, and which go far to deprive us of the monopoly of Russian trade which we formerly enjoyed,—circumstances altogether distinct from the cost of labour and the rate of wages in England.

"First of all, the Continent has the advantage of uninterrupted railway communication with Russia, while our goods have to be chiefly carried by sea during the months of summer. In the case of rolling stock, for instance,

English houses are obliged to be cautious in taking orders for delivery in the autumn of the year. In the second place, the facility of communication with Russia has led to the German manufacturer having greater confidence than his English competitor in Russian customers. He knows the market better, readily takes the bonds of railway companies in payment for rolling stock, is better acquainted with the Russian tariff and Customs regulations, and generally makes it more his study how to push his trade in Russia, offering, as she does, a vast and ever expanding field for his enterprise. In the course of the studies which I have made on the subject of the trade between Great Britain and Russia, I have been very much struck by the want of knowledge that exists in England with respect to the Russian market. Few appear to have cared to enquire seriously whether anything could be done in this country, while their better instructed brethren from Germany and Belgium have been quietly pushing their way. The new tariff and more liberal commercial policy of the Russian Government seem, however, to have aroused the attention of our manufacturers."

Admitting that the progress of continental manufacturers in Russia is not wholly due to their advantages in the price of labour, and that new circumstances have arisen, which must in any case have deprived us of a portion of our former trade, the warnings of Mr. Michell equally deserve the attentive consideration of our workmen and their employers.

Trades Unions must beware.

The competition of the continental manufacturers demands, it is obvious, our close attention. Manufacturers must exercise their best commercial, administrative, and inventive faculties to maintain their position; and the workmen must take care that they do not impede the progress of industry by unreasonable demands, and by attacks upon capital which ample information would have shown to be ill advised.

The good done by Trades Unions.

I have said much about the harm done by the Trades Unions in vain attempts to force up the rate of wages by regulations which tend to destroy the free liberty of the labourer;

for though, in raising wages the Trades Unions can do but little good to the workmen and may do some injury to the masters, in other respects, and especially as benefit societies, the Trades Unions have effected, and are capable of doing, great good to the working people. They encourage a spirit of self-help, and, in point of fact, devote by far the greater portion of their funds to "benefit objects." For example, the Engineers' Society, out of a total income of 49,000*l.*, spends but 724*l.* a-year in contributing to the support of the members of the Unions who are out on strike.

We shall do well to encourage every effort which our working people are making, to ensure themselves against the risk of scanty employment and the degradation of pauperism.

We cannot but honour and admire the sentiments of fraternal sympathy, which prompt men to promote each other's advancement in life by that mutual aid and support which these societies are intended to afford. It may be apprehended that the existence of

CHAP. I.

an organization framed for the purpose of carrying on a strike, may, like the maintenance of large standing armies, be a provocation of war; but if a strike should unfortunately occur, under the control of a Trades Union, the conduct of the workmen will probably be as much superior to that of the rioters in the manufacturing districts in the early part of the present century, as the discipline of a standing army is superior to that of a guerilla band.

Discipline under Trades Unions.

To treat the workman who strikes for higher wages as if he were on all occasions the unprovoked assailant of his master, is unjust. In most cases the presumption is, that the workmen believe that they have a right to claim a concession for which they have—it may be vainly—applied. If they were not convinced of the justice of their claim, and of the ability of their masters to make the concession, the workmen would scarcely be prepared to make the terrible sacrifice which they endure in a long continued strike.

The "Revivers."

During the period of distress in the Isle of Dogs which followed the last commercial panic, the decay of shipbuilding attracted the attention, not only of the employers, but of other enquirers into the circumstances to which it was attributable.

Some employers said that it was chiefly the result of the excessive price of labour. A large number of the workmen, however, alleged that free trade was the cause, and the walls of the deserted workshops were freely placarded with such documents as the following :—

The "Revivers'" address.

"To the Working Men and Women of England. The 'Revivers'' Association will hold their eighth public meeting at the Red Church school room, Bethnal Green Road, on Monday, June 7, 1869, to which those are invited who will conform to the rules of the Association. There will be a few reserved seats for those who feel inclined to pay 6*d.* each to help to pay the expenses. The Chairman of the Association will preside.

"We place before you a few plain questions :—

"Are your wages to be gradually reduced

CHAP. I.

The "Revivers'" address.

"Are you to be out of work, and go into the workhouse or stone yard?

"Are your wives and families to starve?

"Because of the introduction of the products of foreign labour into this country in the shape of foreign manufactures of every kind, and this *without reciprocity.*

"Believe us, friends, this is the true cause of our difficulties and distress, and we warn you that we have not yet seen the bitter end. Let us forget general politics, and look at our material interests—*our business, our trade, our life.*

"Ask your brother workmen all over England—more especially those at Millwall and every ship-building port, at Macclesfield, Coventry, and Spitalfields; at Leek, Preston, Manchester, and Derby; at Nottingham, Congleton, and Sanbach; at Leighton Buzzard, Luton, Newport Pagnell, and Tring; at Exeter and Crediton; in fact, ask all, yourselves included, and you will find that, with a few exceptions, none are now getting a proper living, and we tell you your prospects are gloomy, if you do not put your

CHAP. I.

The "Reviver's" address.

shoulders to the task and demand protection for British labour.

"Remember that the ruin of Ship-building involves about thirty, and that of Watch-making about sixty other trades, and that all are gradually passing away from us. The Iron Trade and Engineering are losing ground. English carpenters' work is superseded by foreign doors, windows, &c., the Lathrenders are done, the Silk and Ribbon Trades are almost gone. Foreign agricultural implements, furniture, and artificial flowers, baby linen, baskets, beads, and beds, Berlin work, hardware, blankets, bonnets, boots, braid, brushes, and buttons, candles, canes, cannon, caps, cardboard, and carpets, china, clocks, cloth, crape, and cutlery, damask, de Laine, electrotype-paper and pencils, fancy goods, fringe, lace, gilded goods, gloves, gold and silver articles, hosiery, leather, linen, looking glasses, lucifers, shoes, silk manufactures, soap, stationery, stays, steam engines, and steel pens. In fact, nearly everything, small or great, is now done by foreigners. What have you left to

CHAP. I.

The "Revivers'" address.

make? Could you not make all those articles here? And if you did so, would any of you be out of employment? No! This, then, is the cause of your distress! And remember that these classes being out of employment destroy the necessity for other labourers. But if all were in full working order, labourers would be fully employed, and every shopkeeper would at once feel the benefit of the expenditures of all these classes; and in fact would be daily extending their business, which is now slack, because no one has any money to lay out simply because they receive no wages. Some of you may be enabled to say that the particular trade in which you are engaged has not yet been interfered with by foreigners, but let them but know it, and you will soon share the same fate.

"The rules of the association are that neither general politics or religion may be discussed. We have had plenty of that lately. Let us like men of sense deal with this vital question fairly and justly.

"Doors open at half-past seven o'clock.

CHAP. I.

The "Revivers'" address.

Chair to be taken at half-past eight precisely. "Free trade a gigantic mistake. A pamphlet one shilling."

We objected very lately to the dictation and bad political economy by Trades Unions, but the remedy proposed by the "Revivers' Association" would be still more fatal to the industry of the country.

The "Revivers" were wrong in their assumption that the shipbuilding business, which had been once conducted with such activity in the Isle of Dogs, had been transferred to foreign ports. Owing to the general depression of commerce, it was languishing everywhere. The shipbuilders of France were not less clamorous for protection than their unfortunate rivals on the banks of the Thames. The "Revivers" desired to secure to the British workmen a monopoly at home. They forgot that if they succeeded in excluding foreign productions, the price of every article of consumption, which had been partly supplied from abroad, must be augmented, and that the increased cost of living would more than neutralize the advantage of

CHAP. I.

The "Revivers'" address.

protection against foreign competition. They forgot that the monopoly of the home market, a limited outlet after all, in comparison with the wide arena of external commerce, would be much too dearly bought if obtained, as it must inevitably have been, at the sacrifice of our export trade.

CHAPTER II.

DEMAND AND SUPPLY.

Wages regulated by demand for labour and supply.

WHETHER we call the regulating power the relation between supply and demand, or, with Mr. Thornton, say, that the power of labour is absolutely under the sway of competition, the power of controlling the rate of wages lies equally far beyond the scope of Trades Union organization. An increase of wages can only take place when trade is prosperous, and when the supply of labour is not sufficient to meet the increasing demand. "When," says Adam Smith, "in any country the demand for those who live by wages is continually increasing, the workmen have no occasion to combine to raise their wages. The demand increases necessarily with the increase of the revenue and stock of every country, and cannot possibly increase without it." . . . . "It is in the progressive state, while a Society is advancing to further acquisition, rather than when it has acquired its full complement of riches, that the condition of the labouring poor, and of the great body of the people, is the happiest and most comfortable. It is healthy in a stationary, and miserable in a declining state. The progressive state is, in reality, the cheerful and the hearty state in all the different orders of society. The stationary is dull, the declining melancholy."

Examples on railways.

These axioms of the great economist are abundantly verified by the practical experience of Railway Contractors. Many interesting examples of the effect of unusual pressure upon the labour resources of a sparse and scattered population, or of a rapidly increased demand, even in the most populous districts, have presented themselves in the course of Mr. Brassey's extensive experience. The advance of wages which has occurred in such cases from the natural operation of the laws of supply and demand, would satisfy the most golden conceptions of the working man.

Wages on the Grand Trunk Railway.

When the Grand Trunk Railway was being constructed in Canada, Mr. Brassey sent out, at his own expense, a great number of operatives from this country. Men were engaged in Lancashire and Cheshire; and, on landing in Canada, received forty per cent. more for doing the same work than they had been previously earning in England. The cost of the works was about thirty per cent. dearer. The wages of labourers were 3*s.* 6*d.* a day at the commencement of the works, and rose to 6*s.* a day ere they were completed. Masons, whose wages when in England were 5*s.* a day, and who were taken out to Canada at the expense of the contractors, earned 7*s.* 6*d.* a day in the colony; although the cost of living was not greater in Canada than in England; but the supply of their labour in England was abundant, while in Canada skilled artisans were comparatively rare.

New South Wales.

For the construction of a railway in New South Wales, two thousand men were sent out from England, at the joint expense of the contractors and the Government. The cost of living for a single navvy was 10*s*. a week; as compared with eight shillings a week in England. But notwithstanding that the difference in the cost of living was so small, and that the whole expense of their voyage had been defrayed by their employers, yet, in consequence of the scarcity of labour in the colony, navvies, who in England had been paid from 3*s*. 3*d*. to 3*s*. 6*d*. per day, received from 7*s*. 6*d*. to 8*s*.; and the wages of skilled hands were increased in proportion. The daily wages of masons ranged from 11*s*. to 13*s*.; bricklayers, 11*s*. to 12*s*.; brickmakers, 8*s*. to 10*s*.; and carpenters, 10*s*. to 12*s*. Such an advance in the rate of pay of the same men can only be explained by the altered relations between the supply of labour and the demand in the colony, as contrasted with the mother country.

Bilbao and Tudela Railway.

In Spain, a few years ago, in the construction of the railway from Bilbao to Tudela, the wages earned by labourers, which, at the commencement of the contract, were one shilling a day, rose, before the works were completed, to three shillings a day. On the same contract, the wages of the masons increased, in the corresponding period, from one shilling and fourpence to five shillings a day.

Effect of panics.

The fall in wages, which follows a commercial panic, when production is diminished and employment is scarce, proves how closely the rate of wages depends upon alterations in the relation between supply and demand. When the panic took place in the railway world in 1847–8, even the common labourers, employed on the Eastern Union Railway accepted lower wages.

Royston and Hitchin Railway.

In 1849, on the Royston and Hitchin Railway, labour was cheaper than it has ever been since. The reduction was a direct consequence of the depression, caused by the collapse of railway enterprise in 1847–8. Men who, on the North Staffordshire line, shortly before the panic, had been paid 3*s.* 6*d.* a day only earned half-a-crown on the Royston and Hitchin line.

Cheshire Junction line.

A member of my father's staff informs me that at the same period and from the same

CHAP. II.

cause, the wages of the navvies, which in the inflation of the railway mania in 1846 had been advanced in some cases to 6*s*. a day, in the collapse following on the panic were so much reduced that on the Cheshire Junction line, the cost of the work was in consequence diminished by not less than fifteen per cent.

Mr. Mackay's Comparative Table of Wages on English Railways, 1843 to 1869.

The following statement gives the weekly wages earned by men employed on railway works from 1843 to 1869. The notes furnish a comparative statement of the cost of work represented by the different rates of wages, and contain a short explanation of the extent of the demand for labour at the different periods included in the Return :—

PERIODS.

	1843	1846	1849	1851	1855	1857	1860	1863	1866	1869
Masons	21/	33/	24/	21/	25/6	24/	22/6	24/	27/	27/
Bricklayers	21/	30/	24/	21/	25/6	22/6	22/6	24/	27/	25/6
Carpenters and Blacksmiths	21/	30/	22/6	21/	24/	22/6	22/6	24/	25/6	24/
Navvies, Getters (Pickmen)	16/6	24/	18/	15/	19/	18/	17/	19/	20/	18/
,, Fitters (Shovellers)	15/	22/6	16/6	14/	17/	17/	16/	17/	18/	17/
Cost of labour only, per cube yard :— . .										
Of Brickwork . .	2/3	3/9	2/9	2/3	2/6	2/6	2/4	2/6	2/9	2/6
Of Earthwork . .	/4½	/7½	/5	/4	/5½	/5¼	/5	5/½	/5¾	/5½

CHAP. II.

Mr. Mackay's evidence on wages paid on English railways.

1843.

"Gloucester and Bristol Railway, period of general depression, provisions for men and horses very cheap. Men plentiful, excellent workmen. Clay cuttings, on the Gloucester to Stonehouse line, taken out at 6*d.* a yard, inclusive of horse labour."

1846.

"Lancaster and Carlisle, Caledonian, Trent Valley, North Staffordshire, Eastern Union Railways in construction. Height of the railway mania. Demand for labour excessive, very much in excess of supply. Beer given to men as well as wages. Look-outs placed on the roads to intercept men tramping, and take them to the nearest beershop to be treated and induced to start work. Very much less work done in the same time by the same power. Work going on night and day, even the same men working continuously for several days and nights. Instances recorded of men being paid for forty-seven days in one lunar month. Provisions dear. Excessively high wages, excessive work, excessive drinking, indifferent lodgings caused great demoralisation, and gave the death-blow to

CHAP. II.

the good old navvy already on the decline. He died out a few years after this period."[1]

Mr. Mackay's evidence on wages paid on English railways.

1849. "Great Northern, Oxford, Worcester and Wolverhampton, Oxford and Birmingham, Chester and Holyhead Railways, in construction. Great reduction in wages caused by the financial embarrassments in October 1847, and political turmoils and revolutions in 1848 on the Continent and at home. General distrust, aggravated by the unsettled state of affairs abroad. Works stopped in 1847, partially resumed in 1848. The 1846 contracts not yet completed. In 1849 work comparatively plentiful. Provisions moderate in price."

1851. "Shrewsbury and Hereford, North Devon, in construction. Contracts taken in 1846 now all completed. Great depression in the labour market. But little work going on. Political affairs on the Continent unsettled. Provisions very cheap."

1855. "Leicester and Hitchin, Leominster and Kingston Railways in construction. Work

[1] Other experienced contractors do not admit that good navvies can no longer be obtained.

Mr. Mackay's evidence on wages paid on English railways.

still very slack during this period. Best men gone to France, Spain, Belgium, Switzerland, and Italy to Mr. Brassey's works. Crimean War, militia all called under arms. These circumstances tended to raise wages. Provisions dear, horse provender excessively high, costing 5*s*. a day each horse."

1857.

"Shrewsbury and Crewe, Leominster and Kingston Railways in construction. Work still very slack; the effects of the Crimean War had not wholly passed away."

1860.

"Knighton and Craven arms, Woofferton and Tenbury, widening of Shrewsbury and Hereford, Severn Valley Railway works in construction. Men plentiful, provisions cheap."

1863.

"Tenbury and Bewdley, South Staffordshire, Ludlow and Clee Hill, Wenlock, Nantwich and Drayton, widening of Shrewsbury and Hereford, Worm Valley drainage, Letton Valley drainage in construction. Men plentiful, provisions rather dear."

1866.

"Wellington and Drayton, widening of Nantwich and Drayton, Hereford Loop,

CHAP. II.

Mr. Mackay's evidence on wages paid on English railways.

1869.

Hooton and Parkgate, Wenlock and Craven arms, Ebbw Vale in construction."

"Silverdale and Drayton, Sirhowy, widening of Abergavenny, and Merthyr Railways, and London drainage works in construction. Provisions rather dear."

The explanatory memorandum does not exhaust the list of Mr. Brassey's contracts in progress at the several dates mentioned. Those contracts only are included which happened to be in the recollection of the writer, whose immediate field of observation was necessarily limited to a few contracts in the Midland Counties.

It will be observed that the fluctuations in the rate of wages exhibited in the return take place in exact conformity with the law of wages as stated by Mr. Ricardo when he says: "The market price of labour is the price which is really paid for it, from the natural operations of supply and demand. Labour is dear when it is scarce, and cheap when it is plentiful."

Effect of the

The unusual pressure on the labour market, during the continuance of the Crimean War,

Crimean War on wages.

produced a marked effect on the rate of wages in every trade, both in England and on the Continent. In the construction of the Bellegarde Tunnel, two and a half miles in length, on the Lyons and Geneva Railway, the wages of the Piedmontese quarrymen rose from 2½ to 3, 3½, and 4 francs a day; and the Englishmen, who were employed in the tunnel, working in shifts of from six to ten hours each, were paid at the rate of from 8 to 10 francs a day. Their wages were raised, partly on account of the difficult nature of the works, some idea of which may be formed, when it is mentioned that the shafts were from 600 to 700 feet deep; but the general rise of wages consequent upon the Crimean War had a still greater influence in determining their pay.

At Woodford, in Essex, the wages of navvies rose to 6*s.* a day, at about the same period and from the same cause.

Rise of wages in Europe from increased activity of trade.

Our operatives have but a faint conception of the rise of wages which has taken place abroad in countries where Trades Unions did not exist, and where the improvement in

CHAP. II.

the workman's condition was attributable solely to the increased demand for labour. From the tables given in the report prepared by Mr. Phipps, on the Industrial Classes in Wurtemberg, it appears that the average increase in the rate of wages, in eight branches of manufactures and industry, during the last thirty years, amounted to between sixty and seventy per cent. In the building trades the rise of eighty to ninety per cent. is to be explained solely by the unusual activity in the trades. As a general average sixty-nine per cent. may be taken as the increase in the daily wages for the out-door labourers. In their class the increased demand for labour is peculiarly noticeable.

In Hungary.

In Hungary, before 1865, the wages of common labourers were 1*s.* 3*d.* a day. In Moldavia the same rates of wages were paid on the railways, although agricultural labourers were earning only 6½*d.* a day in money, together with an equivalent of 3½*d.* in food.

In Saxony.

In 1871, in Saxony and Bohemia, in consequence of the great and increasing demand for labour, both on the railways, and from the general revival of industry after the cessation of hostilities with Prussia, the daily wages of labourers rose to 2*s.* and 2*s.* 6*d.*

In Moldavia.

On the Suczawa Line, the wages of labourers, at the commencement of the works, varied from 45 to 60 kreutzers, or 9*d.* to 1*s.* a day; but, owing to the demand for men on the Moldavian lines, the wages rose within a year to from 60 to 80 kreutzers, or 1*s.* to 1*s.* 4*d.* a day.

Rise of wages in Silesia.

A work by Herr Jacobi, quoted by Mr. Petre, describes the remarkable advance in the rate of wages in Lower Silesia. The rates have doubled generally within the memory of the older workmen; and, in particular cases, the recent rise has been sudden and great. At Loben, in Silesia, it is said that the erection of a factory in an agricultural district caused a rise in labourers' wages, which were only 6*d.* a day for men, and 3*d.* for women—to the extent of 100 per cent. for the latter, and 50 per cent. for the former: a most remarkable illustration of the effect of the altered relation between the demand for labour and the supply.

CHAP. II.

Rise of builders' wages in London from increased demand.

The advance in wages in the building trades in London has been considerable; but it has been the necessary result of the altered relation between the supply of workmen and the demand for labour.

The Metropolitan Railways, the growth of Kensington, Bayswater, and other suburbs, are visible evidences of the pressure of the demand of the builders of London upon the supply of labour in the trades which they employ.

Abundant evidence in support of this explanation of the cause of the rise of wages in all branches of trade is supplied by employers by no means friendly to the Trades Unions.

Mr. Trollope's evidence.

Mr. Trollope, for example, made the following admission in his evidence before the Commissioners: "I am bound to say that hitherto there has been such an enormous pressure for work, that almost every man who can handle a tool has been taken on at an unreasonable rate."

Mr. Mackay's evidence.

Again, speaking of the advance in wages in the building trades in the provinces, Mr.

Mackay, a member of my father's staff, observes in a Report he has made to me on the subject: "Wages have risen, during the last twenty years, from twenty to twenty-five per cent.; but by the force of circumstances they would have risen as much or more if Trades Unions had never existed."

Same cause produces same effect in cases of boiler makers.

To the same effect Mr. Robinson, the Managing Director of the Atlas Works, Manchester, said in his evidence before the Trades Unions Commissioners: "I do not think the Unions have altered the rate of wages; the changes are rather due to the demand for labour in particular branches. Between 1851 and 1861 no advance took place in the wages of the engineers, though theirs is the most powerful of the Trades Societies; but, in the case of the Boiler Makers, wages rose from 26*s.* to 32*s.* 6*d.*, in consequence of the extension of iron ship-building, and the great amount of iron-bridge work."

Limits within which fluctuations take place.

The rate of wages cannot long continue so high as to deprive capital of its fair return. For if it did, capital would seek some other

CHAP. II.

investment of a more satisfactory nature. Neither can the rate of wages long continue below the amount necessary to maintain the labourer and his family. The fluctuations in the rate of wages between the two limits, depend entirely upon the varying demand for labour.

Recent fluctuations and advance caused by altered conditions of Trade.

We see this principle of political economy fully illustrated at the present time. Why are the columns of our newspapers filled with accounts of strikes and trade disputes? Why are the working men in every branch of manufacturing industry making ever new demands for an increase of wages, or a reduction of hours—which is only an increase of wages in another form? It is because labour has become comparatively scarce.

On the Kensington and Richmond line, shortly before the last panic, the men had become almost unmanageable; but immediately after the failure of Messrs. Overend and Gurney, their tone was changed and their demands were much more reasonable.

The recent increase in the demand for labour has produced a marked effect upon the rate of wages on the Wolverhampton and Walsall Railway. Three years ago the navvies were paid at the rate of 2*s.* 9*d.* a day. Their wages are now from 3*s.* 6*d.* to 3*s.* 9*d.* a day; and no more work is done for the money. Excavation is being made at a cost of 7*d.* a yard, which was thought to be dear work when the cost was about 4½*d.* a yard. The explanation of the present high rate of wages, is to be found in the fact that the railway in question is in the centre of the colliery districts, where the demand for labour in the collieries has caused a corresponding rise of wages for the workmen on the railway. Drivers, engaged at regular standing wages at the rate of a guinea a week on the Wolverhampton and Walsall Railway, are being attracted into the collieries by an advance of wages to the rate of 4*s.* 6*d.* a day. The same causes are producing the same effects on the Continent as in England. In Brussels such is the demand for labour for excavation, that the men employed as navvies are actually receiving higher wages than skilled masons. The wages of the navvy in Brussels are 60

CHAP. II.

centimes an hour, whereas the masons are receiving only 50 centimes.

The industrial history of past years, so admirably reviewed in the columns of the 'Economist,' furnishes a striking illustration of the rise of wages consequent upon the activity of trade.

In 1871 wages rose in the iron, engineering, coal, and hardware trades from fifteen to twenty per cent. In the Cleveland iron trade the rise was even greater. The wages of labourers advanced from 3*s.* to 4*s.* a day; puddlers from 40*s.* per week to 55*s.*; and from 5*s.* 3*d.* to 7*s.* per score of 7½ tons.

Agricultural labour in demand in Lancashire factories.

In Lancashire and Yorkshire labour is so scarce that lads are now being imported from the country into the cotton trade. Their wages commence at from 15*s.* to 16*s.* per week. The exports from the United Kingdom last year reached the value of 319,000,000*l.*, and the greatest increase took place in those trades in which the wages had advanced the most. Our exports of iron and steel have actually doubled within the last seven years. If, therefore, the wages of puddlers and colliers have gone up, the advance was fully explained upon the strict principles of political economy.

The activity of the Welsh iron manufacture at the present time is unprecedented. The rise in wages in the iron manufacture in the north of England, during the past year, has already been given. The following statement, which has been kindly prepared for me by the proprietors of large iron works in South Wales, shows the comparative earnings of the workmen in their employ, in the years 1842, 1851, and 1869 (see next page) :—

When capital is enjoying so much prosperity, who shall grudge to labour a liberal participation in the profits of business? I have no sympathy with the aggressive and restrictive spirit of Trades Unionism; but surely every fair and generous mind must rejoice that the condition of the labourer is improved.

High wages in Colonies due to insufficient supply of skilled labour.

Owing to the limited supply of skilled labour, the wages of artisans in all newly settled countries are high as compared with the rate prevailing in England. A fitter,

Comparative Earnings of Workpeople employed in Iron Manufacture.

	1842.		1851.		1869.	
Occupation.	Price per ton.	Wages per week.	Price per ton.	Wages per week.	Price per ton.	Wages per week.
Miners . . .	—	10/ to 16/	—	11/ to 16/	—	12/ to 18/
Colliers . . .	—	14/ to 16/	—	15/ to 18/	—	16/ to 20/
Furnaces :—						
Founders .	/4	17/ to 18/	/3	25/ to 29/	/1 8/10	27/ to 30/
Fillers . .	,,	17/ to 18/	,,	25/ to 29/	,,	27/ to 30/
Cinder fillers	/3½	15/ to 16/	/2½	21/ to 24/	/1 2/10	20/ to 22/6
Labourers .	—	10/6	—	10/6	—	11/6 to 12/6
Forge :—						
Puddlers	Pig-iron, nil Metal, 5/6	Share. 16/ to 16/6	Pig-iron, 4/10 Metal, nil	Share. 16/ to 18/	4/11 and 5/11 4/	Share. 18/ to 24/
	1st hand	21/ to 22/	1st hand	22/ to 25/	1st hand	28/ to 32/
Labourers .	—	10/6	—	10/6	—	10/6 to 13/
Girls . . .	—	nil.	—	4/9	—	5/6 to 6/6
Mills :—	Bar-iron		Rails.		Rails.	
Heaters . .	1/5	24/ to 26/	First heater, 1/1 Second heater, /6½	25/ to 27/ 35/ to 37/	First heater, /10½ Second heater, /5¼	25/ to 28/6 35/ to 40/
Rollers, &c.	1/8¼ contract	—	/10¼	—	/7¾	Roller, 50/ Rougher, 40/ ea.
Labourers .	—	10/6	—	10/6	—	11/ to 12/6
Girls . . .	—	4/9	—	4/9	—	5/6 to 8/
Carpenters . .	—	12/6	—	13/ to 14/	—	13/ to 16/6
Pattern Makers	—	13/ to 14/	—	13/	—	13/6 to 19/
Fitters . . .	—	12/ to 14/	—	12/ to 14/	—	13/ to 19/
Blacksmiths .	—	12/ to 15/6	—	Contract	—	14/ to 22/6
Masons . . .	—	12/ to 15/	—	15/	—	14/ to 20/

CHAP. II.

Argentine Republic.

whose wages in England would be 30*s*. a week, commands a salary of 200*l*. a year at Rosario in the Argentine Republic. The engineers of the steamers on the River Plate, all of whom are Englishmen, are paid at the rate of from 16*l*. to 20*l*. a month, or more than double the rate at which they would be paid in England.

Nor is this difference in the rate of wages confined to skilled artisans; even the least skilled description of labour is highly paid in countries in which the supply of labour falls short of the demand. In the Argentine Republic the wages of a farm labourer range from 6*s.* 8*d.* to 8*s.* 3*d.* a day.

So in half-civilized countries. Persia.

So in other parts of the world. One of the last investigations made on my father's behalf was connected with a project for a complete system of railways in Persia. If the scheme had been carried out, it was assumed that the pay of engine-drivers, fitters, and station-masters, would be 250*l.* a year, and of foremen platelayers 120*l.* a year.

Syria.

In Syria the rates of wages are higher than might have been expected—not indeed because capital is abundant, but because the supply of labour is limited. In Alexandretta the daily wages of common labourers are 1*s.* 4*d.*; masons and carpenters are paid from 2*s.* 7*d.* to 3*s.* 7*d.* a day. In Aleppo the daily wages of masons are 2*s.* 3*d.* to 2*s.* 9*d.*; carpenters, 2*s.* 2*d.* to 2*s.* 7*d.*; masons' labourers, 1*s.* 10*d.*, and masons' boys, 1*s.* 3*d.*

CHAP. II.

InColonies where climate is unfavourable.

When labour is scarce in a colony in which the climate is unfavourable to the development of the physical powers of European workmen, and where the cost of living is high, there seems scarcely any limit to the rates of wages. I will take, as an example, the earnings of the operatives in Lima, where in 1869 machinists received 10*s.* 6*d.* to 18*s.* per day; boiler makers and smiths, 12*s.* to 18*s.* a day; plumbers, 10*s.* 6*d.* to 15*s.*; common labourers, 3*s.* 9*d.* to 6*s.* With regard to the cost of living, single men can board at Lima for from 2*s.* 3*d.* to 3*s.* a day, and the rent of houses, containing two or three rooms and a kitchen, varies from 2*l.* 5*s.* to 3*l.* 15*s.* a month.

The figures quoted from the Report of the English Consul show what high wages are offered in Peru to European artisans. The navvy appears to be in still greater demand. A certain number of navvies have been sent over from England lately to act as foremen upon the works of the Callao Docks now in progress. Their wages have been fixed at 8*s.* a day; but Mr. Meigs, an American contractor for some Peruvian railways, induced the men to leave the Docks, and enter into his employment on the railway by offering them the apparently preposterous sum of 22*s.* 6*d.* a day. The men could not resist so great a temptation. From causes, however, which have not yet been explained, the occurrence having only recently taken place, they remained but a short time on the railway, and returned to the less lucrative employment on the docks much disgusted with their experience of railway employment in Peru.

High wages in United States and from scarcity of skilled labour especially in Western States.

In the United States the wages of skilled workmen average from 9*s.* to 15*s.* a day, and those of unskilled workmen from 2*s.* 6*d.* to 7*s.* 6*d.* It cannot be supposed that so great a difference between the reward of labour on the opposite shores of the Atlantic is due to the superior organization of Trades Unions in the United States. In New England there are powerful combinations among the artisans, but none among the agricultural labourers, yet, as compared with the same class in England, the condition of the com-

CHAP. II.

mon labourer is, of all others, the most improved by emigration to America. And let it be observed that, as agriculture is the most flourishing, so it is the most important of all the industries of the United States. The value of the total annual production of the leading industries has been estimated by Mr. Wells at 1,365,000,000*l*. To this total, agriculture contributes 685,590,000*l*. The demand for labour to bring under cultivation the vast tracts of land still unoccupied is such that it has never yet been satisfied. Hence a rise of wages in strict conformity with an economical law.

Wages at Buffalo.

In the recent report of Mr. Hemans, the British Consul at Buffalo, the wages of the working classes in that city are given as follows: "Per day, skilled artisans, 16*s*. to 24*s*.; carpenters, 6*s*. to 14*s*.; masons, 10*s*. to 16*s*.; unskilled labourers, 4*s*. to 6*s*.; and dock labourers, 12*s*. to 16*s*."

Wages in California.

The wages in California are higher than in any other State of the Union; because the expense of a journey to the remotest limits of the Western Continent has hitherto prevented a supply of labour from keeping pace with the demand. "Under these circumstances, the condition of the artisans and the industrial classes," says Consul Broke, "has been one of unparalleled prosperity. The following table gives the rates of wages in the building trades at San Francisco: Bricklayers, 20*s.* per day of 8 hours; plasterers, 16*s.* per day of 8 hours; stonemasons, 18*s.* to 20*s.* per day of 8 hours; hod-carriers, 15*s.* a day of 8 hours."

The completion of the Pacific Railway has not yet affected the labour market in California; but it is certain that it must tend in the long run to equalise the value of labour in the Western and the Eastern States.

Rise of wages in India.

Since 1853 we have subscribed no less than 40,000,000*l.* for India Railways. A considerable portion of this sum has been paid to native labourers, and the result has been that in the districts traversed by these railways, wages have advanced within a short time no less than 100 per cent. In consequence of the great demand for work-

CHAP. II.

men, the price of labour has increased to an extent still more marvellous in Bombay.

Wages in that Presidency are now two or three times higher than in Bengal and the Punjaub.

Sir Bartle Frere's evidence.

In a paper furnished to the Select Committee on East India Finance by Sir Bartle Frere, some remarkable examples are given of a rise in wages in consequence of the increased competition for labour for railways and other great public works.

The following table shows the variations in the average monthly wages of a carpenter in Bombay :—

1830–39	1840–49	1850–59	1863
s. d.	s. d.	s. d.	s.
30 4	28 10	32 7½	58

The following table shows the wages of a coolie at the same periods :—

1830–39	1840–49	1850–59	1863
s. d.	s. d.	s. d.	s. d.
14 9½	12 3½	14 2	27 0

Effect of railway

Everywhere in the vicinity of railway works the collectors remark on their great works in India.

effect in raising wages. The practice of promptly paying for all labour in liberal money wages caused an important social revolution in the habits of all who live by labour, even at a great distance from the railway works. The labourers often travelled from their homes 200 miles to obtain work so paid, returning home at the harvest-time.

The people of the Abruzzi came up in thousands to work for six months in the winter season, on the Maremma Railway, and returned home in a precisely similar manner for the harvest. It is interesting to observe how similar was the influence of the same circumstances on two nations geographically remote, but not very far removed from each other in the scale of civilization.

The increase in wages in Bombay had increased the number of consumers of superior qualities of grain and meat. The increased consumption had raised the cost of living. The advance in the cost of living had had the effect of raising the rate of wages: for with their former earnings the

CHAP. II.

people could no longer have provided them selves with the necessaries of life.

Moreover, the increased external trade of Bombay, the influx of money for the purchase of commodities and the consequent depreciation in the purchasing power of bullion, and the increased demand for labour, had by their combined influence produced an astonishing advance of wages in Bombay, as compared with Bengal.

Wages in Bengal and Bombay.

The following table shows the difference between the rates in Bengal and Bombay :

	In Bengal per month.	*In Bombay per month.*
	Rupees.	Rupees.
Carpenters	9	25
Masons	$5\frac{5}{16}$	21
Labouring Coolies	6	$9\frac{10}{16}$
Horse-keepers	5	$8\frac{9}{16}$

It is impossible to produce a more striking example of the effect of an increased cost of living, and an increased demand for labour in raising the rate of wages.

In a country in which the erroneous policy of protection is still adopted by the Government, the price of labour, from the increased demand for it, will advance, as might be expected, in a still more rapid ratio than in a country in which a free trade policy is adopted. The closing of the home markets in Russia to foreign trade, is producing a sensible effect on wages and the cost of living. I quote the following from Mr. Michell: "It is fortunate that such an amelioration of the condition of the people is taking place." In many districts black bread and water are the only food of the people, and the cost of this meagre dietary varies from 5*s.* to 6*s.* a month. Owing to the extension of railways, the rate of wages and the style of living are happily improving even in the remoter districts. The chief articles of consumption have risen, in the last ten years, from thirty to fifty per cent., but the rates of wages have increased in an equal, and in many cases, in a greater, proportion.

It is evident from the results of the large experience of many employers, from which the cases which have been enumerated have been taken, that at all times, in all places, and under all circumstances, a rise of wages will take place whenever the demand for labour increases more rapidly than the supply, and that no increase can take place, except under that condition.

Pernicious in their social tendency and scientifically inaccurate are the doctrines of those who seek to persuade the working people that the capitalists are their natural enemies. This latter opinion is well explained by Bastiat, in his "Harmonies Économiques," from which the following lucid exposition is extracted:—

"Le capital, jusqu' où qu'il porte ses prétentions, et quelque heureux qu'il soit dans ses efforts pour les faire triompher, ne peut jamais placer le travail dans une condition pire que l'isolement. En d'autres termes, le capital favorise toujours plus le travail par sa présence que par son absence.

"Rappelons-nous l'exemple que j'invoquais tout à l'heure.

"Deux hommes sont réduits à pécher pour vivre. L'un a des filets, des lignes, une barque et quelques provisions pour attendre les fruits de ses prochains travaux. L'autre n'a rien que ses bras. Il est de leur intérêt de s'associer. Quelles que soient les conditions de partage qui interviendront, elles n'empireront jamais le sort de l'un de ces deux pêcheurs, pas plus du riche que du pauvre, car dès l'instant que l'un d'eux trouverait l'association onéreuse comparée à l'isolement, il reviendrait à l'isolement."

The people of England are happily without experience of the condition to which the labourer is reduced in countries in which the invigorating influence of capital is unfelt. But there are isolated communities even in Europe, in which the low estate of the people affords a melancholy example of the results of that separation of capital from labour to which Bastiat refers.

Bothnia.

At the head of the gulf of Bothnia, far removed from the enjoyments and advantages of European civilization, there dwells a community of peasants, on whose dreary abode for a considerable part of the year the sun never shines. In frost, and snow, and darkness, throughout their long winter, these unfortunate people are engaged in felling and sawing timber, and making tar. When the spring at length returns, and the seas so long frozen up are once more navigable, a few mercantile agents pay them an annual visit and purchase the timber and the tar which have been prepared in the previous winter. The purchase is effected, not by giving money in exchange, but by a system of barter, in which the peasants, innocent of the value of their own labour, are hardly dealt with. They receive a supply of meal barely sufficient to maintain them during the coming winter, and a limited quantity of cast-off clothing, purchased perhaps, from the old clothes dealers of London. Many of these poor people have never tasted meat, and as they are always in debt to the merchants for the supplies of meal which they have accepted in advance, they are not in a position to negociate, as independent parties to the transaction, for more liberal terms of payment.

During the summer the people work for a great many hours; but, from imperfect nourishment, their physical strength does not

CHAP. II.

enable them to put forth the same exertions as an English workman. To what shall we mainly attribute their pitiable condition? To the entire absence of accumulated capital, and the dependance of the peasantry on employers who are too poor to be generous, and in whom the desire to make the most of their small capital has altogether extinguished the virtue of charity and the spirit of justice.

CHAPTER III.

COST OF LABOUR CANNOT BE DETERMINED BY THE RATE OF WAGES.

CHAP. III.

Cost of labour cannot be determined by rate of wages.

IT is said by a numerous section of employers that the cost of labour has risen in this country to a point far beyond anything which has been attained in the corresponding trades on the Continent; and they allege a difference in the rate of wages, as if that were conclusive evidence that their apprehensions are reasonable. But I maintain, unhesitatingly, that daily wages are no criterion of the actual cost of executing works, or of carrying out manufacturing operations. On the contrary, experience teaches that there is a most remarkable tendency to equality in the actual cost of work throughout the world. In the industries which compete against the manufactures of the Continent for the supply of the neutral markets of the world, it is clear that Trades Unions cannot raise the cost of production in this country beyond the cost of producing an equivalent quantity of work abroad, without diminishing the relative rate of profit of the British manufacturer; and that if the rate of profit which could be obtained by an investment of capital at home were to be reduced below the profit accruing from a corresponding investment abroad, the immediate result would be the withdrawal of capital from this country. In point of fact, the amount of daily wages affords no real measure of the actual cost of work; and it is quite possible that work may be more cheaply executed by the same workmen, notwithstanding that their wages have largely increased. I proceed to give evidence in support of this opinion.

Amount of wages no criterion of work.

North Devon Railway.

At the commencement of the construction of the North Devon Railway, the wages of the labourers were 2*s*. a day. During the progress of the work their wages were raised to 2*s.* 6*d.* and 3*s.* a day. Nevertheless, it was found that the work was executed more cheaply when the men were earning the higher rate of wage than when they were paid at the lower rate. Again in London, in carrying out a part of the Metropolitan Drainage Works in Oxford Street, the wages of the bricklayers were gradually raised from 6*s.* to 10*s.* a day; yet it was found that the brickwork was constructed at a cheaper rate per cubic yard, after the wages of the workmen had been raised to 10*s.*, than when they were paid at the rate of 6*s.* a day.

Drainage Works, London.

Russia.

In Russia the nominal price of labour is lower than in any other country in Europe; yet the manufacture of iron is at least as costly in Russia as in England; and it is considered politic by the State to give an artificial encouragement to the iron manufacturers by paying a bounty of 4*l.* per ton on all rails made in the country. Cases to prove that the actual cost of labour cannot be measured by the rate of daily wages can be indefinitely multiplied from railway experience.

In making the South Staffordshire Railway, the navvies employed by Mr. Day, my father's resident agent, were paid from 3*s.* to 3*s.* 6*d.* a day. A few years later, Mr. Day was engaged on the construction of a line from Enniskillen to Bundoran; and on that line the labourers were paid at the rate of 1*s.* 6*d.* to 1*s.* 8*d.* a day. Yet, with this immense difference in the rate of wages, sub-contracts on the Irish Railway were let at the same prices which had been previously paid in South Staffordshire.

Enniskillen and Bundoran.

It is interesting to find these views enunciated by Mr. Joseph Hume in a speech on the Combination Laws, delivered in the House of Commons on June 29, 1825; and to see how correctly his language describes the result of my father's experience. He said that he had heard it stated "that low wages were a good thing. That he denied. Low wages tended to degrade the labourer. It was the high wages which the English artisan received, compared with the miserable pay of the Irish labourer, which made the former so superior in energy."

Mr. Joseph Hume.

CHAP. III.

Report of Irish Railways.

The inferiority of the Irish labourer in the days of Mr. Hume is described and fully explained in the Report of the Irish Railways Commissioners presented to Parliament in 1837: "In the northern province the people were better lodged, clothed, and fed, than in the other provinces; the wages of labour were higher, being, on the average, about 7*s.* a day; and their food consisted chiefly of meal, potatoes, and milk."

Labour in the South of Ireland.

"In the southern districts the food of the population was inferior, consisting at best of potatoes and milk, without meat. The wage of the labourer varied from 1*s.* to 8*d.* a day. But the condition of the inhabitants of the western district was inferior even to that of the people of the south of Ireland. Their food consisted of potatoes alone, without meal, and, in most cases, without milk. The cabins were wretched hovels, their beds were of straw, and the wages of the labourer were reduced to the lowest point, being, upon the average, not more than 6*d.* a day." We shudder as we read this description, and anticipate the inevitable consequences.

Poverty and misery had deprived them of all energy. Every motive to exertion was destroyed; agriculture was in the rudest and the lowest state.

Effect of low wages.

The effect of these depressing circumstances, aggravated of course by the backward state of agriculture, was strikingly illustrated in the deficiency of produce and in the amount of work performed by Irish labour, compared with that of the same class in England.

The Irish Poor Law Commissioners stated that the average produce of the soil in Ireland was not much above one half the average produce in England, whilst the number of labourers employed in agriculture was, in proportion to the quantity of land under cultivation, more than double, viz., as five to two. Thus ten labourers in Ireland raised only the same quantity of produce that four labourers raised in England, and this produce was generally of an inferior quality. So striking a disproportion, though generally admitting of very considerable qualification with reference to the different

CHAP. III.

nature and degree of facilities afforded to the labourer in the two countries, still shews a decided advantage in favour of the English workman, and goes far to prove the dearness of ill-requited labour.

I wish to establish my position on this subject by adducing the testimony of manufacturers, who have had experience in spheres which lie beyond my own immediate observation; and on this ground I would refer to a speech delivered by Sir Francis Crossley, in a debate on the appointment of the Trades Unions Commission in 1867, in which he expressed very just and generous views on the relative value to the employers of well-paid and ill-paid labour. "There was," he said, "a good deal of unreasonable feeling abroad; that it was wrong for working men to sell their labour at the best price, but it must be remembered that their labour was the only thing that they had to sell; and the best thing to do was to leave these matters to take their natural course. It was a great mistake, on the part of employers, to suppose that the lowest priced labour was always the cheapest. If there were not so much desire to run down the price of labour, and the masters showed a more conciliatory spirit, there would be fewer strikes and outrages."

Warwickshire labourers.

The condition of the Warwickshire labourer has of late been brought prominently under the notice of the public. The internal economy of the agricultural labourer's household has been minutely described in the columns of the "Daily News." I would ask men of business to examine this question, not from a philanthropic point of view, but for the purpose of ascertaining what rate of wages will give the best return to employers.

Rent.

It is quite true that the rent received by the English landlord gives but a miserable return on the capital value of his property. In no country indeed does landed property give so poor a return. It is equally certain that the business of farmers is not as lucrative as that of manufacturers. If the agricultural labourer receives higher wages without doing more work in the day, the farmer and landlord will suffer a diminution of income, which they can ill afford to bear; and the only

CHAP. III.

result will be that capital will be withdrawn from agriculture, and more advantageously invested in other business. But are we justified in assuming that the labourer is incapable of doing more work for a more liberal reward? I will not be so presumptuous as to offer an opinion upon the particular case of the Warwickshire labourers; but this I say, that all experience shows that, with proper supervision, and with an equitable scheme of prices for piece work, the best paid workman does more work for a given sum of money than the underpaid and therefore under-fed labourer can by possibility accomplish. The cost of labour, rightly observes Mr. Fawcett, "is determined by the amount of work which is really done for the wages. Many of our labourers can barely obtain the necessaries of life; and we can all appreciate the false economy that would be practised, if a horse was so much stinted of food that he could only do half as much work as he would be able to perform if he were properly fed."

High wages do not necessarily imply dear

Uniform cost of labour.

labour, just as, on the other hand, low wages do not, of necessity, make labour cheap. On my father's extensive contracts, carried on in almost every country of the civilized world and in every quarter of the globe, the daily wage of the labourer was fixed at widely different rates; but it was found to be the almost invariable rule that the cost of labour was the same—that for the same sum of money, the same amount of work was everywhere performed. Superior skill, extra diligence, and a larger development of physical power, will often compensate the employer who finds himself obliged to pay higher wages than his competitors. On the other hand, if labour becomes so costly in England that our productions are undersold by the foreigner, our customers will leave our markets, and the workmen's livelihood will be lost.

General uniformity in cost of labour.

It is extremely difficult to compare accurately the whole cost of production of any class of goods in England and abroad. The daily wage, it has been shown, is not the true measure of cost. The superior diligence, the skill and energy of the workmen, may and generally do largely compensate the employer who pays a higher rate of wages. Or again, when the superior qualities of the operatives do not fully make up for the difference in wages, the high price of labour will generally lead to the use of labour-saving machinery, which would not have been adopted had labour been cheap. Our labour is expensive; indeed, with the greater cost of living in this country, it could not but be more expensive than it is abroad. But we have on our side the many great qualities of our operative population; the large resources, the fruit of many years of thrift and patient toil, at the command of our capitalists; the abundant supply of fuel; and the admirable faculty of organization which is the distinguishing feature of English industrial economy. With these advantages, and by dint of strenuous efforts, we have hitherto held our own amid an increasing number of competitors. In some branches of trade we are behind; in others, and in probably the greater number of the more important trades, we are still in front. In machinery, and in textile manufactures of the cheaper kind, and in most branches of metallurgy, we are slightly in advance of the Continent; but even where we are still ahead, our rivals follow closely at our heels.

We encounter severe competition in every branch of trade.

In some parts of the Continent a railway can be made at a less cost than in the more expensive districts in England. There is but little difference in the cost, and none in the quality, of an English, French, or a German locomotive, made by the best manufacturers of each country. The Trades Unions should be mindful of these things. Extravagant demands on behalf of labour may destroy the old industrial supremacy of this country; and a concession may be dearly bought if, in the end, the employment of the British workmen is transferred to his foreign rival.

General appreciation of situation best formed by lookers on at a distance.

While I venture to give this warning, I feel no present alarm. The workman and his master, like soldiers in the thickest of the fight, who see only their immediate opponents and nothing of the general combinations of the battle, are each disposed to exaggerate the power and importance of the other. In order to form a more correct judgment, we must withdraw to a distance from the battle-field, and in a serener atmosphere we shall be better able to measure the strength of the contending forces. We shall find, as we examine the industrial situation, that the labour market is sensitive to every fluctuation of trade, that the price of labour rises with the demand, and falls when the competition among the employers for the services of workmen becomes less keen.

Once duly impressed with this great economical truth, we may listen with unruffled patience to the allegations which, in times of commercial depression, are invariably made, that our trade has gone to other countries, because the wages of the British workman are excessive.

So long as the cost of production in this country exceeds the cost of production in other countries, the neutral markets of the world will no longer draw their supplies from England. The demand for labour here will accordingly diminish: the multitudes of people out of employ will be driven, under the pressure of necessity, to compete against each other for employment; wages will thus be in proportion diminished, until we are once more in a position to compete. The difficulty which we apprehend will, in exact proportion to its gravity, bring its own appropriate remedies. *Solvitur ambulando.*

Paris and Rouen Railway.

I will now give an interesting example, derived from my father's early experience in France, in the construction of the Paris and Rouen Railway in 1842. The Paris and Rouen Railway was the first large railway work executed on the Continent. About 10,000 men were employed in its construction, of whom upwards of 4,000 were Englishmen. Perhaps so remarkable an exodus of English labour to continental Europe never before occurred, and it is improbable that it will ever be repeated. A special effort was made to secure the services of English workmen on this particular contract; because it was a question whether native workmen could be obtained in suffi-

CHAP. III.

cient numbers, and it was still more doubtful whether they would possess the necessary skill and experience for carrying out railway works, which at that period were a novelty, even to English engineers, and entirely unknown on the Continent. Under these exceptional circumstances, a large body of Englishmen were sent over to Normandy.

The responsibility of taking so large a body of Englishmen into a foreign country was very serious; but the greatest efforts were made by the contractors to mitigate the inconveniences to the English workmen of residence in a foreign country They originated schools, and provided the spiritual succour of two or three clergymen.

Medical staff.

They also organized a system of medical attendants. The Rouen line was divided into districts, and one English physician was appointed as superior medical attendant for the whole of the works; and he placed, at certain distances apart, resident surgeons to attend upon the sick and wounded, and also upon the wives of the workmen. It is scarcely necessary to observe that the employment of English manual labour abroad must always be costly, and a somewhat doubtful policy. But in this particular case it was not found to be disadvantageous in a pecuniary point of view.

The contract for the Paris and Rouen line included some difficult works. There were four bridges across the Seine, and four tunnels, one of them one mile and five-eighths in length, passing through hard limestone. The English were chiefly employed on the difficult work. The French labourers drew away the stuff, or wound it up the shafts; but the mining was done by Englishmen. In the tunnels the skilled work was all done by them. At one time there were five hundred Englishmen living in the village of Rollebois, most of whom were employed in the adjacent tunnel. Although these English navvies earned 5*s*. a day, while the Frenchmen employed received only 2*s*. 6*d*. a day, yet it was found, on comparing the cost of two adjacent cuttings in precisely similar circumstances, that the excavation was made at a

CHAP. III.

lower cost per cubic yard by the English navvies than by the French labourers.

Wages at Bonnières.

In the same quarry at Bonnières, in which Frenchmen, Irishmen, and Englishmen were employed, side by side, the Frenchmen received three francs, the Irishmen four, and the Englishmen six francs a day. At those different rates, the Englishman was found to be the most advantageous workman of the three.

On the completion of the Paris and Rouen line, and the extension to Havre, most of the English navvies returned to their own country; and the Dieppe line was executed principally by native labour, although Englishmen were still employed on the more difficult work. On the Dieppe Railway French labourers earned from two and a half to three francs a day; and, when working by piece work, their earnings advanced to three and a half francs a day. The wages of Englishmen, employed as plate-layers and tippers, were about five francs a day. A large number of Belgians were employed on this contract, and they always earned one franc a day more

CHAP. III.

than the Frenchmen. It should, however, be explained that the construction of railways had been considerably developed in Belgium before railway works were commenced in France. Upon the Caen line, which was executed about ten years later than the Dieppe line, Englishmen were still employed for tipping and plate laying, and on difficult work in the deep rock cutting. The wages of the Englishmen were five francs a day as before; while the usual earnings of the French labourers ranged from 2·75 to 3 francs and 3·50 francs a day. It is to be noted that the English workmen were employed by sub-contractors, whose interest was directly involved in the closest possible reduction of expenditure. Yet those most experienced practical men were of opinion, that the English were worth the much higher rate of wages which they received, when employed on a work of exceptional difficulty.

Caen and Cherbourg Railway.

I may mention, as an illustration of the benefits invariably conferred by railways upon the rural districts in which they have been constructed, that in the districts adjacent to

CHAP. III.

Wages near Caen.

the Caen line, the average wages for agricultural labourers were 1·50 franc a day. The same men, who were employed on the railway, received from 2 francs to 2·25 francs and 2·75 a day.

I have elsewhere shown the difference that exists between the wages of the industrial classes in England and France. That difference was much greater twenty-five years ago; but, in spite of the advance of wages, France is better able to compete with us than in former days when her labourers were much less liberally paid. Twenty-five years ago large quantities of English rails were imported for the Rouen and Havre line, though at that time the duty amounted to 5*l.* per ton.

General comparison.

Extending the investigation to other contracts in France, and to Italy, Austria, Switzerland, Spain, Germany, Belgium, and Holland, it has been found that there is hardly any perceptible difference in the cost of railway work, executed by unskilled labour, although the difference in the rates of the daily wages prevailing in those countries is most striking. The wages paid in this country are higher than in any other. Yet even with respect to bridges, viaducts, tunnels, and all works of art on railways, they can be executed at a cheaper rate in England than in any other country in the world. The rate of wages is much lower, but masonry costs as much in Italy as in Manchester. This approximate uniformity of cost is exhibited in all cases. The superiority of the Englishman to the workmen of other nations was equally remarkable, whenever there was an opportunity of employing him side by side with them. The wages of the Dutchmen engaged in the construction of the Dutch Rhenish Railway, varied from 1*s.* 6*d.* to 1*s.* 8*d.* a day, when paid by the day. At piece-work they could earn 2*s.* or 2*s.* 6*d.*; but good workmen from the Lancashire fens would have made 3*s.* 6*d.* at similar work.

The Dutch.

Both English and French masons were employed in large numbers on the Alderney Breakwater in 1852. The Englishmen earned 5*s.* 6*d.* to 6*s.*, and, as a general rule, they made 1*s.* a day more than the Frenchmen,

Alderney.

CHAP. III.

whose average earnings did not exceed 4*s.* a day.

It has been many times stated in the course of this work that from superior skill or greater energy, the more highly paid workman will in many, perhaps in most, cases turn out a greater amount of work, in proportion to the wages he receives. An opportunity occurred some years ago, during the construction of the refreshment room at Basingstoke, for testing this problem with great accuracy. On one side of the station a London bricklayer was employed at 5*s.* 6*d.* a day, and on the other two country bricklayers at 3*s.* 6*d.* a day. It was found, by measuring the amount of work performed, without the knowledge of the men employed, that the one London bricklayer laid, without undue exertion, more bricks in a day than his two less skilful country fellow labourers.

Grand Trunk Railway.

On the Grand Trunk Railway a number of French-Canadian labourers were employed. Their wages were 3*s.* 6*d.* a day, while the Englishmen received from 5*s.* to 6*s.* a day;

but it was found that the English did the greatest amount of work for the money. The same remarkable tendency to equality of cost exhibits itself even in India. On the Delhi and Umritzir Railway it has been found, as I am informed by Mr. Henfrey, my father's resident partner in India, that, mile for mile, the cost of railway work is about the same in India as it is in England; although the wages, if estimated by the amount of daily pay, are marvellously low. Earthwork, it is true, is executed by the coolies at a cheaper rate than in England, but native skilled labour is more expensive.

Delhi and Umritzir Railway.

The wages paid on the Delhi and Umritzir Railway were: Masons, 10 to 12 rupees a month; carpenters, 15 to 18; bricklayers, 8 to 12. The execution of the works on a railway in India is generally undertaken by small contractors or middle men, who in many cases are shopkeepers. There is a difficulty in obtaining experienced sub-contractors, and in consequence it is necessary to employ a numerous body of English foremen. Hence

CHAP. III.

the cost of supervision is greatly enhanced in India, and is found to amount on the average to twenty per cent. on the entire outlay.

Standard of living.

Before the railways caused an increased demand for labour in India, wages ranged from 4*d.* to 4½*d.* a day. The demand for labour raised wages considerably, but even then the coolies were not paid more than 6*d.* a day. However these wages far more than sufficed to supply all their wants. Their food consists of two pounds of rice a day, mixed with a little curry; and the cost of living on this, their usual diet, is only 1*s.* a week. For 1*s.* 6*d.* they can live in comparative luxury. On the railways of India it has been found that the great increase of pay which has taken place, has neither augmented the rapidity of execution, nor added to the comfort of the labourer. The Hindoo workman knows no other want than his daily portion of rice, and the torrid climate renders watertight habitations and ample clothing alike unnecessary. The labourer therefore desists from work as soon as he has provided for the necessities of the day. Higher pay adds nothing to his comforts; it serves but to diminish his ordinary industry.

Eastern Europe.

In Eastern Europe the standard of living is very low, and the earnings of the labouring people are scanty in proportion. The Galicians live principally upon black bread, schnapps, a spirit distilled from Indian corn, and potatoes. The inhabitants of Bukovina and Moldavia live on Indian corn and schnapps, at a cost of from 4*d.* to 5*d.* a day. Ninepence may be considered the ordinary wages for labourers in this part of the country. The peasants are very improvident. When the Indian corn crop fails, they literally starve; and in the winter they are obliged to obtain advances from the proprietors, or from Jews, undertaking to work out these allowances in the course of the following summer. When bound by an engagement such as I have described, their wages are reduced to 6*d.* or 7*d.* per day. In Moldavia and other European countries similarly placed in the scale of civilization, unskilled labour is cheaper than in England; but, in proportion as skill and manual dexterity are required,

Uniformity of cost.

CHAP. III.

the differences in the cost of constructing engineering works disappear.

Italy.

In Italy, as in India, it has been found that a numerous but unskilled population, in a climate where the necessaries of life are inexpensive, can undertake the mere manual labour at a cheaper rate than in England; though this is only true when works are not pushed on so rapidly as to require the importation of labour from a distance. When the local labourers are alone employed, the Italian villagers, men, women, and children, carrying earth to and fro in baskets on their heads, and as ignorant as the Coolies themselves of the resources and appliances of mechanical science, can execute earthwork about as cheaply as in India. On the other hand, masonry and other work requiring skilled labour is rather dearer in Italy than in England.

Mauritius.

In the Mauritius the result of the experience acquired in the construction of a railway in that island by my father's partner, Mr. Longridge, established the same result as in the cases already quoted. Though the daily wages are low, yet when you take into account the extra supervision, the cost of earthwork, rock cutting, and masonry, is quite as great as the cost in England; and skilled work, as, for example, carpentry, is from twenty to twenty-five per cent. more costly in the Mauritius than it is in England.

Other occupations.

I turn from the business of the railway contractors to other occupations: and in whatever sphere of industry, where equally complete investigation is made of the actual cost of production, as compared with the rate of wages, I arrive at a similar result. The shipbuilders at Bordeaux, Marseilles, and Nantes, who appeared as witnesses before the committee appointed to conduct the "Enquête sur la Marine marchande," under the presidency of M. Rouher, described in accents of despair the collapse of their industry in France, and the impossibility of competing in point of price with the English shipbuilders.

English ship-builders have successfully

It is certain that the stationary if not the retrograde condition of French ship-building is not attributable to the difference in the

CHAP. III.

competed with the French; though wages in England are much higher.

rate of wages in favour of the British ship-builder.

Tableau comparatif du prix du Travail dans les ateliers de construction des services maritimes des Messageries impériales.

PROFESSIONS	GAGES JOURNALIERS	
	1859	1869
Modeleurs	4·08	4·47
Ajusteurs	3·69	3·80
Chaudronnerie de cuivre	3·34	3·90
Chaudronnerie de fer	2·73	3·70
Forgerons	3·27	3·80
Charpentiers	3·22	3·99
Maçons	2·89	3·99
Manœuvres	2·74	2·99
Menuisiers	3·64	4·00
Perceurs	4·29	4·90
Calfats	3·40	3·90
Voiliers	3·40	3·90
Scieurs de long	4·08	3·89
Bateliers	4·08	3·89

If the French table of wages be compared with the following statement of the average rate of wages paid at Millwall from 1863 to 1866, it is marvellous that any ships should have been built in the Thames for Mediterranean ship owners :—

	s. d.	s. d.	
Wood Shipwrights		7 0	per day.
Joiners		6 0	,,
Platers	6 8 to	7 0	,,
Riveters		5 4	,,

CHAP. III.

	s.	d.		s.	d.	
Chippers . . .	5	0	to	5	6	per day.
Smiths				6	0	"
Hammermen . .	3	9	to	4	0	"
Plumbers				5	6	"
Painters				5	0	"
Engineers . . .	5	8	to	6	0	"
Pattern makers				6	0	"
Moulders				6	4	"
Labourers				3	6	"
Boys . . . from	4	0	to	15	0	per week.

There must be a remarkable superiority either in vigour or in skill in the English workman or he could not have held his own in the race in spite of the extraordinary difference in the rate of wages. The cost of provisions is an essential element in determining the wages of the labourer, but the standard of comfort which the working classes are content to adopt, has also a most material influence on their condition. Mr. McCulloch attributes the difference between the condition of people in England and Ireland mainly to the different standard of living adopted by the people themselves.

Wages depend on the standard of comfort.

The rate of necessary wages must vary with variations of climate, and other things

On climate.

being equal, it will be the highest in countries where the most expensive clothes and houses and the largest supplies of fuel are required.

There is a maximum limit above which wages cannot rise, and a minimum below which they cannot fall. The minimum is determined by the cost of living according to the standard adopted by the people. Wages cannot long continue below the amount necessary for the support of the labourer and his family. On the other hand, wages cannot long continue so high as to deprive the employer of a fair return upon his capital, and a reasonable reward for the application of his time and abilities to the conduct of his business. If wages exceed the maximum limit determined by the necessity of fulfilling the conditions enumerated, capital will no longer be embarked in undertakings from which no adequate return can be obtained.

There is a remarkable instance of high wages, in consequence of the cost of living being artificially raised, at Beyrout. Every inhabitant is taxed 4*l.* a-year for the supply of water. Owing to the pressure of this taxation, the wages of common labourers are from 2*s.* to 2*s.* 6*d.*, and of masons and carpenters 3*s.* to 4*s.* a day.

On the cost of food.

"It is not," says Mr. McCulloch, "in the best situated countries, or those of which the climate is the finest and the soil most productive, that the peasantry are the best off. In those their necessities are few and easily supplied, and when these are satisfied, they seem to care for nothing more." Humboldt tells us that it had been proposed to prohibit the culture of the banana in Mexico, as being the only means calculated to rouse the torpid qualities of the natives and make them in some degree industrious.

Ill-paid workmen are ill fed, and were deficient in physical power.

As we recede from the more civilized countries of Europe the standard of comfort is reduced, and the labourer is content to receive lower wages; although in most cases the amount of work performed is diminished in corresponding proportions. High wages and short hours of work may not be found incompatible with a diminished cost of production; and low wages and long hours may

CHAP. III.

sometimes prove less advantageous to the employer than shorter hours of labour and a higher rate of wages. This apparent anomaly is partly explained by the necessity of giving to the labourer, who has to undertake severe manual exertion, the means of procuring a generous diet. In Belgium the workmen are not so expensive in their habits as the English artificer. They consume less meat; their bread is seldom purely wheaten; and they work for lower wages; but, on the other hand, it cannot be expected that, under these conditions, they can have the same physical vigour as the English labourers, who are better fed.

Mr. Hewitt, to whose evidence I have elsewhere referred, speaking on this subject, remarked that at Sireuil the rate of wages of the common labourer will only admit of his having meat once a week; and yet the manufacturers were not making money. He also stated that there was a deplorable look of hopelessness among the lower class of workmen at Creuzot, though this was not discernible among the better paid men.

Observations of Montesquieu.

It is interesting to observe how fully the experience of practical men bears out the opinion expressed by Montesquieu, in the "Esprit des Lois," "Il y a dans l'Europe une espèce de balancement entre les nations du Midi et celles du Nord. Les premières ont toute sorte de commodités pour la vie et pour les besoins; les secondes ont beaucoup de besoins et peu de commodités pour la vie. L'équilibre se maintient par la paresse qu'elle a donnée aux nations du Midi, et par l'industrie et l'activité qu'elle a données à celles du Nord."

Mr. Lothian Bell, Mr. Wells, and Mr. Redgrave on the cost of labour.

The recent interesting publications of Mr. Lothian Bell, a report to Congress of Mr. Commissioner Wells, the Special Commissioner of Revenue in the United States in 1868, and a report of Mr. Redgrave, one of the Inspectors of Factories, contain many other equally remarkable cases in various trades, all tending to prove that the cost of labour cannot be conclusively determined by the rate of daily wages in the respective industries.

Mr. Lothian Bell's

Mr. Lothian Bell, in an address read at a meeting of ironmasters in the North of

CHAP. III.

enquiries in France.

England, gave the result of his investigations as to the cost of smelting pig iron in France, which distinctly proved that more men were required to do the same quantity of work in France than in England. He stated that, by a very careful enquiry at a large establishment in France, he had ascertained that forty-two men were there employed to carry out the same amount of work which twenty-five men were able to do at the Clarence factories on the Tees. In spite of the actual labour on a ton of pig iron for smelting being twenty per cent. cheaper in France than in England, the entire smelting charges were sensibly greater in France than in the general run of work at Middlesbrough. And, taking into account the saving in respect of fuel, the cost of producing pig iron in France was twenty shillings, in some cases even thirty shillings per ton more than that exhibited by the cost-sheets of the manufacturers at Cleveland.

Coal.

The average cost of raising coal at the pit's mouth in France is said by Mr. Lothian Bell to be from 5*s.* 6*d.* to 6*s.* a ton, and the average price of coal 11*s.* per ton; the price for small coal used by the ironmasters being 8*s.* 6*d.* as compared with 5*s.*, the price paid by the Cleveland smelters.

CHAP. III.

Belgium; cost of getting coal.

Belgium raises 11,000,000 tons of coal annually, and exports 4,000,000 to France. The average cost of coal at the pit's mouth is from 5*s.* 6*d.* to 7*s.* a ton. The price varied in 1867 from 9*s.* 6*d.* to 10*s.* 6*d.* a ton. It is clear from these figures that neither in France nor in Belgium is the cost of extracting the coal reduced by the low price of labour. In the manufacture of iron, the opinion of Mr. Bell is confirmed by Mr. Hewett, an American ironmaster, who told the Trades Unions Commissioners, that the price of iron was 1*l.* sterling per ton higher at Creuzot than in England, and by M. Michel Chevalier, who, in his introductions to the Reports of the Jurors of the French Exhibition in 1867, said that rails were from twenty-five to thirty francs dearer per ton in France than in England. A similar difference was shown in the rails purchased for the Mont Cenis Railway, the price of which at the works in France was from 7*l.* 12*s.* to 8*l.* per ton; while

Mr. Hewett confirms the statement of Mr. Bell.

Price of rails in France and England.

CHAP. III.

the price in England was 7*l.* per ton. The duty of 2*l.* 8*s.* per ton which is still payable on rails imported into France is a proof of the conscious inability of the French iron-masters to compete with our manufacturers in an open market.

Cost of production in German ironworks.

In Germany as in France, though the nominal rates of wages are still lower, the actual cost of the work is greater than it is in England. Mr. Lothian Bell observed that, whereas labour in Westphalia cost from twenty to twenty-five per cent. less than with us, the labour-saving arrangements were much neglected; and a ton of iron smelted in the Ruhrort district could not be produced for less than 15*s.* a ton above the cost upon the Tees.

Mr. Wells on the cost of puddling.

Mr. Commissioner Wells, in an able report to the American Congress, has discussed in minute detail this most important question of the comparative cost of labour in the principal manufacturing countries. Taking the puddling of iron as the representative process of the iron trade, he says that he found that the average price of labour per day for puddlers was from 7*s*. 6*d*. to 7*s*. 10*d*. in Staffordshire; 6*s*. 4*d*. in France; and from 4*s*. 9*d*. to 5*s*. in Belgium; yet the average price of merchant bar-iron was 6*l*. 10*s*. in England, 7*l*. in Belgium, and 8*l*. in France.

Mr. Redgrave on the cost of spinning.

In a recent report on the condition of the textile industries in England, Mr. Redgrave, one of Her Majesty's Inspectors of Factories, says that, while the foreigner is under the same conditions, as to the raw material, as the English manufacturer, and his fuel is more expensive, his workpeople do not work with the same vigour and steadiness as Englishmen. Consequently, the same number of operatives, employed upon the same machinery, do not produce the same quantity of yarn as in this country. "All the evidence that has come before me," he says, "has gone to prove that there is a great preponderance in favour of this country. Comparing the work of a British with a foreign spinner, the average number of persons employed to spindles is—in France, one person to fourteen spindles; in Russia, one to twenty-eight spindles; in Prussia, one to thirty-seven; in Great Britain, one to seventy-four. But I could find many cotton spinning factories in my district, in which mules containing 2,200 spindles are managed by one minder and two assistants. "I have recently been told," he continues, "by one who had been an English manager in a factory at Oldenburgh, that, though the hours of work were from 5.30 A.M. to 8 P.M. every day, only about the same weight of work was turned off under English overlookers as would be produced in a working day from 6 A.M. to 6 P.M. in this country. Under German overlookers the produce was much less. The wages were fifty per cent. less in many cases than in England; but the number of hands, in proportion to machinery, was much larger. In some departments it was in the proportion of five to three. In Russia the inefficiency of the labour of the foreign, as compared with the labour of the English operatives, is even more strikingly manifested, for on a comparison of the wages, supposing the Russian operatives to work only sixty hours a week as they do in England, instead of seventy-five as they do in Russia, their wages would not be one fourth the amount earned in England. But the wage must be taken into account with the power of the operative as a producer; and herein will be found an advantage of the English operative over the foreign competitor, sufficient, with some qualification, to counterbalance the mere cheapness of wage."

Mr. Wells on the cost of spinning.

Mr. Wells, in the report to which I have already referred, confirms the view expressed by Mr. Redgrave. He says that, "whereas female labour in the cotton manufacture is paid at from 12*s.* to 15*s.* a week in Great Britain; at from 7*s.* 3*d.*, to 9*s.* 7*d.* in France, Belgium, and Germany; at from 2*s.* 4*d.* to 2*s.* 11*d.* in Russia; the one thing which is most dreaded by the continental manufacturers everywhere is British competition. The demand for protection is loudest in France, Austria, and Russia, where the average wages reach their minimum."

Russian mowers—Mr. Mill.

Mr. Mill in his "Political Economy" quotes a statement made by Professor Jones, in which he said that the Russians, or rather those German writers who have observed the

CHAP. III.

manners and habits of Russia, supply some remarkable facts: "Two Middlesex mowers," they say, "will mow in a day as much grass as six Russian serfs, and in spite of the dearness of provisions in England and their cheapness in Russia, the mowing of a quantity of hay, which would cost the English farmer half a copeck, will cost the Russian proprietor three or four copecks." The Prussian Councillor of State, Jacobi, is considered to have proved that in Russia, where everything is cheap, the labour of the serf is doubly as expensive as that of the labourer in England. In Austria the labour of a serf is one-third of that of a free hired labourer.

Women employed as field labourers in the less civilised countries.

The miserable pay of the women employed in the manufactories of Russia suggests some observations as to the evils which necessarily arise from subjecting the female population to excessive manual labour. In all the less civilised countries of Europe the women are compelled to share in the manual labours of the men. This practice is in a large degree the cause of that very poverty which it is intended to alleviate. The introduction of so many additional hands into the labour market has a marked effect in diminishing the reward of labour. On the Lemberg and Czernowitz line, in some places, half the people employed were women. They earned 1·60 franc a day, and the men from 2 to 3 francs a day.

On the Bukovina line the wages of the men for picking were 1*s.* 6*d.* per day, while the women, who worked only with the shovel, earned about 6*d.* a day less than the men. The cost of living for a man and his wife and three children in Hungary, may be stated approximately at 1*s.* a day. In those countries the cost of unskilled labour is small, but the struggle for life is so severe that every child, the moment it can add the smallest fraction to the earnings of the family, is sent into the fields. The sacrifice of these earnings, however scanty, for a few years, for the purpose of acquiring a knowledge of a skilled trade, is impossible with a peasantry so destitute; and the cost of skilled labour is thus disproportionately high, because so

Skilled labour disproportionately dear in a poor country.

few persons possess the means of passing through a period of unpaid apprenticeship.

Misery of the Russian peasantry.

An apprehension of the military power of Russia, which a certain school of politicians are too ready to entertain, might, perhaps, be changed to pity if they knew the condition of the Russian peasantry, as described by Mr. Michell, and their inability to bear the strain of a long-protracted war. Even in peace they are engaged throughout their lives in an exhausting struggle for bare existence. From abject poverty the women are compelled to share unceasingly in the out-door labours of the men. The infant mortality in Russia is appalling. The peasant women of Russia give birth to their offspring under circumstances equally perilous to the life of the mother and the child. Their confinement takes place in a barn or a stable. They have no medical attendance, and in three days at the utmost they are once more employed in hard field labour. The result of such privation and suffering is, that a large proportion of infants die within a week after their birth. The number of males living at

CHAP. III.

Duration of life.

the age of five years, in proportion to the total number of the population, is 20¾ per cent. less in Russia than in Great Britain, France, and Belgium. The shortness of the average duration of life in Russia is equally lamentable. In the North-West Provinces, the average limit of life is between twenty-two and twenty-seven. In the Volga basin and South-Eastern Provinces it is twenty years. In Viatka, Perm, and Orenburg, it is only fifteen years.

In Great Britain the number of men and women alive between fifteen and sixty, out of 1,000, averages 548; in Belgium 518; in Russia only 265. Hence it may be inferred what difficulty there would be in recruiting an army in the case of a long-continued and sanguinary war.

The spectacle of a vast population exposed to such privation, must awaken the sympathy of every friend of humanity. There is more reason to pity the hard lot of the Russian people than to fear their military resources. What a cruel mockery it would seem to the millions of Russian peasants,

CHAP. III.

whose lot in life is so depressed compared with that of the very humblest of our labourers, if by chance it reached their ears that there were statesmen in England who believed that the most imminent danger of their own more favoured land was the growing power of the Russian Empire!

Miserable pay of the Russian labourer.

In Russia the day labourer's wages range from 8*d.* to 1*s.* 4*d.* with food, the cost of which is from 2*d.* to 3*d.* a day. The average pay of the female labourer is 6½*d.* a day, with the addition of food. During harvest, the male labourer can command from 1*s.* 4*d.* to 2*s.* 8*d.* a day with food; the female labourer from 9½*d.* to 2*s.* 8*d.* a day with food. What is the result of this low-priced labour, as compared with other European countries, in which much higher wages are given? The yield of crops in Russia is said by Mr. Michell to be less than half the yield obtained in England or Saxony; and smaller than in any other country in Europe.

The impossibility of determining the actual cost of labour by the nominal rate of wages is as fully demonstrated by the experience of the ship owner as by that of the manufacturer.

The cost of working a ship cannot be determined by the rate of wages for seamen.

The wages of shipwrights and the pay of seamen are much more moderate in France than with us. Yet the cost of building ships is ten per cent. greater in France than in England; and the wages of a French crew, in consequence of their greater number, involve an expenditure for manning twenty-five per cent. greater than the corresponding expense in an English ship. I quote these figures from a recent Report by Mr. West.

If, on the other hand, we compare the cost of manning an American ship, with the cost of manning an English ship, we shall see how our comparatively cheaper labour makes us more prodigal in the use of it. The average proportion of seamen in an English ship is one man to every fifteen tons; in an American ship, it is one man to every twenty-five tons.

The wages in England are higher than in any other country in Europe; but it is

It is remarkable that the English manufacturers, who pay a higher rate of wages for the labour they employ than their foreign competitors, can compete most successfully with the rest of the world in point of cheap-

CHAP. III.

in the cheapest class of goods that our superiority is most conspicuous.

ness of production. English travellers in the East, who have examined the European goods displayed in the bazaars of Beyrout and Damascus, will have been pleased to discover an English stamp on every bale of cotton goods. These fabrics were invariably of the cheapest quality. It is solely by our lower prices that we have secured the monopoly of the Syrian market.

CHAPTER IV.

THE INDUSTRIAL CAPABILITIES OF DIFFERENT NATIONS COMPARED.

CHAP. IV.

The industrial capabilities of different nations compared.

THE examples which have been quoted might be indefinitely multiplied; but sufficient evidence has, it is presumed, been given, to prove that the English manufacturer has no grave reason to complain of the position which he occupies in regard to the cost of labour in this country.

The industrial genius of the English workman, though not in all respects equal to that of our foreign competitors, exhibits so many solid qualities that there seems to be as little ground for complaint as regards workmanlike abilities as there is to be dissatisfied with the rate to which wages by an ever increasing

CHAP. IV.

demand on the part of employers, have gradually been raised.

Mr. Kitson.

Mr. Kitson, of Leeds, in his evidence before the Select Committee on Scientific Instruction in 1868, stated that in 1864, in consequence of a dispute with the workmen at Leeds, he had engaged several Frenchmen and Belgians. This experiment proved that "the foreign workmen were scarcely as intelligent as our own." "We are not," he said, "inferior in the manufacture of iron, machinery, and steel, to the foreign iron-masters. The English are equal to the Belgians in the manufacture of iron, and are superior in the manufacture of machinery."

Belgian iron manufacture.

At the locomotive building works in Belgium the work is rarely executed with the same precision as in England. All the parts of English engines, made from the same pattern, are interchangeable. This is not always the case in Belgian engines. Again, the necessity of competition with the foreign trade has somewhat lowered the quality of the Belgian rails, which are occasionally worn out in two years. Previously to the recently restored activity in the iron trade, loud complaints were heard of the difficulties arising from foreign competition ; and especial apprehension was expressed of the danger to British industry from the close competition of the Belgians.

Lord Howard de Walden on Belgian arms.

In an interesting report on Belgian industry Lord Howard de Walden has remarked that the Belgians exhibit their greatest qualities in the manufacture of arms at Liège. "In all works in sheet iron, for example stoves, the Belgians excel ; but in wrought iron they are behind many other countries. A good lock and key is nowhere to be found. It is cheaper to buy one of English make. A tolerable horse-shoe is nowhere to be seen, nor are the agricultural implements of good quality, and yet in carriage building they have been eminently successful."

Superiority of the English as practical mechanics.

Speaking generally, it may be affirmed that as practical mechanics the English are unsurpassed. The presence of the English engineer, the solitary representative among a crew of foreigners of the mechanical genius of his country, is a familiar recollection to

CHAP. IV.

Consul Lever.

all who have travelled much in the steamers of the Mediterranean. Consul Lever, in his report of 1870 from Trieste, says that, in the vast establishment of the Austrian Lloyds at that port, a number of English mechanical engineers are employed, not only in the workshops, but as navigating engineers in the company's fleet. Although there is no difficulty in substituting for these men Germans and Swiss at lower rates of payment, the uniform accuracy of the English, their intelligence, their consummate mastery of all the details of their art, and their resources in every case of difficulty have entirely established their superiority.

Efficiency of labour compared.

The building and working of steamers involves expenditure in almost all descriptions of labour—the purchase of raw materials of every kind, as well as the most elaborate machinery.

The statistics relating to shipping exhibit a marvellous increase in our steam merchant navy as compared with the steam-propelled shipping of any other nation. Go into any port of the Baltic or the Mediterranean ; and the heart of every patriotic Englishman will rejoice in the spectacle of our undisputed maritime preponderance. The returns of the traffic through the Suez Canal afford an equally convincing proof of our maritime ascendancy in every particular.

Englishmen the best miners.

The industrial capabilities of Englishmen are conspicuously shown by their superior skill as miners. Mining is perhaps the most exhausting and laborious of all occupations. It has been found that in this description of work the English miner surpasses the foreigner all over the world. On the Continent, long after earthwork and all the other operations involved in the construction of railways had been committed to the native workmen, English miners were still employed in the tunnels. A few years ago, in making the railway from Chambery, in Savoy, to the foot of Mont Cenis, Piedmontese were employed in the comparatively easy work of tunnelling in the dry rock; but Englishmen were still required to conduct the far more difficult operations in the soft and yielding clay subject to a constant influx of water.

CHAP. IV.

Opinion of Mr. Mill as to the qualities of English as workmen.

The differences of character and capabilities, which tend in such a remarkable degree to establish an equality in the cost of labour in every part of the world, have occupied the attention of many thoughtful and penetrating minds. Mr. John Stuart Mill says that "individuals or nations do not differ so much in the efforts they are able and willing to make under strong immediate incentives, as in their capacity of present exertion for a distant object, and in the thoroughness of their application to work on ordinary occasions. This last quality is the principal industrial excellence of the English people. This efficiency of labour is connected with their whole character, with their defects as much as with their good qualities. The majority of Englishmen have no life but in their work—that alone stands between them and *ennui*. The absence of any taste for amusement or enjoyment of repose is common to all classes. The effect is that where hard labour is the thing required, there are no better labourers than the English."

In point of manual skill, the French and

English are probably equal. In invention the Frenchman may be the cleverer of the two. But in the power of throwing energy into his labour, the Englishman is the better man. I have been told by Mr. Alexander, who has had considerable opportunities of studying the capabilities of French operatives, and who was engaged in superintending the construction of the engines for the short-lived Fell railway over Mont Cenis, that if a Frenchman has a good model of a machine, he will make it as well as an English mechanic, but the same number of English workmen will turn out sixteen machines, when an equal number of Frenchmen would make only four.

The English more energetic and persevering than the French mechanics.

It may be gathered from the experience obtained on my father's continental contracts, that, as a general rule, the superiority of English workmen was most conspicuous when they first commenced work in a country in which no railways had been previously constructed. The inexperience of the French in large engineering works is proved conclusively by the fact, that the works on the Paris

Frenchmen soon acquired skill in the construction of railways.

and Rouen line having been divided into ten separate contracts, for each of which a separate tender was made, in every case the tender of Messrs. Brassey and Mackenzie was fifty per cent. under the lowest tender of the French contractors. Increased experience enabled the French workmen to earn higher wages, and, on the other hand, closer contact with men of less vigorous habits, in some cases, gradually diminished the energy of the English labourers. But on the whole, wherever the English have been employed on the Continent, they have received much higher pay than their fellow workmen, the natives of the country; and the difference in the pay has been fully represented by their superior skill and marvellous energy.

Great pains were taken to ascertain the relative industrial capacity of the Englishman and Frenchman on the Paris and Rouen line; and, on a comparison of half-a-dozen pays, it was found that the capacity of the Englishman to that of the Frenchman was as five to three.

It would however be a mistake to suppose

that the Frenchmen failed to profit by the lessons of experience which they acquired from the temporary introduction of English labour into their country. For ordinary work, Frenchmen soon became almost as efficient as Englishmen, as the following dialogue with Mr. Milroy, a most experienced member of my father's staff, very clearly explains :—

"*Q.* In the particular work you have been speaking of, the two great trades employed were masons and carpenters ?" Mr. Milroy: "Yes, I found plenty of good masons and carpenters in France. The latter are, in my opinion, superior for such works to English carpenters, both in the quality of the work done, and in the price at which they do it. Their tools also are particularly well adapted to the work. This may arise from Paris having been, in a great measure, built of timber, filled in between with small rubble stones and stucco, and then plastered outside. They seemed to have acquired a specialty for that work, and could do it better than any carpenters I have ever seen. What I have stated was proved in 1853, when I went back.

CHAP. IV.

I then went on to the Caen and Cherbourg line. There was only a sprinkling of Englishmen then. The agents and sub-contractors, who went out with me, had acquired the language sufficiently, when formerly engaged in France, to carry on their communications with the French workmen without interpreters. Upon the Paris and Rouen line we had a large proportion of English labourers, but on the Caen and Cherbourg line a very small proportion; yet the one line was constructed quite as cheaply as the other."

Professor Levi on the qualities necessary for industrial success.

It may be interesting to supplement the experience of the railway contractor, by stating the views of acknowledged authorities who have studied these questions in other spheres of industry. Professor Leone Levi, in a paper on the silk manufacture, remarks that in the processes, the manufacture, and cost of material, the different countries of Europe are on a par. The wages of labour in this manufacture are very low, both in England and in other countries; and if they are a little higher here than elsewhere, that is probably more than made up by our superior power of productiveness. It is not indeed by starving the labourer, or by employing cheap and inferior labour, that British manufacturers will ever be able to meet competition. On the contrary, the most prominent want in an industry so light and delicate is a higher class of labourer, more educated, more refined in taste, and even more expert in manual dexterity. The prosperous maintenance of the manufactures in any country mainly depends on the natural facilities and advantages which the nation may possess for it, and on the energy, aptitude, and skill, displayed by the manufacturers themselves. It has already been pointed out that we are not so much behind the Continent in practical science as we are in taste.

The labouring class in France not better educated than in England.

In France, according to a report from the Minister of War in 1866, 30 conscripts out of every 100 were unable to read. In 1864, 2,271 workmen were employed in the establishment of MM. Dollfus, at Mulhausen. Of those not more than 1,553 could read and write.

Technical education more

Technical education, however, is comparatively unimportant to the

CHAP. IV.

essential to employers than workmen.

workman, who has merely to superintend the motion of the machine; although it is certain that if he were of an inventive turn of mind, he might often suggest valuable improvements. But technical education is essentially necessary, and inventive genius is invaluable, in the man who has the superintendence of 100 machines.

The genius of English manufacturers administrative rather than inventive.

In original conception, English manufacturers do not perhaps possess any advantage over the manufacturers of other countries; but in the practical development and application of an invention, and in general administrative capability, and especially in the art of economical management, they have shown a real commercial genius which is rarely exhibited abroad.

CHAPTER V.

DEAR LABOUR STIMULATES INVENTION.

CHAP. V.

The use of machinery has enabled us to compete with dear labour against low wages.

OUR successful competition with other countries is maintained in a large degree by our more extensive use of machinery. In truth it is only by these means that our more highly paid artisans are able to hold their own in the industrial contest in which they are engaged. Nor can it be doubted that the dearness of labour must necessarily give a stimulus to inventive genius which, with a cheaper supply of labour, will probably not be developed in the same degree.

It may be thought that the substitution of machinery for hand labour, and the diminution in the number of hands employed in proportion to the quantity of goods produced, is a change not altogether beneficial to the interests of labour; but it must be admitted that in manufacturing industry the English could no longer have competed successfully with the Continent, unless the cost of production had been continually reduced by mechanical contrivances. It cannot be doubted that it was better for the working man that economy should be obtained by improvements in mechanism and in methods of working than by constant reductions of wages.

M. Michel Chevalier truly says that machinery can alone enable dear labour to compete with cheap labour, and that England, which makes 57 per cent. of the textile fabrics of Europe, owes her superiority entirely to the extensive use of machinery. The economy obtained by the introduction of machinery is often very remarkable. In their gallant struggles in the difficult times following the war in America, our manufacturers developed the resources of machinery to a greater extent than had ever been attempted before, and they succeeded in making a considerable reduction in the amount of labour employed. The results are shown in the subjoined table, taken from a paper read by Mr. Elijah Helm before the Manchester Statistical Society in 1868 :—

CHAP. V.

Statistics of Factories employed in the three great Textile Manufactures of the United Kingdom in the years 1856, 1861, *and* 1868.

	No. of Factories			No. of Spinning Spindles			No. of Power Looms			No. of Persons Employed		
	1856	1861	1868	1856	1861	1868	1856	1861	1868	1856	1861	1868
COTTON FACTORIES:												
England and Wales	2,046	2,715	2,405	25,818,576	28,352,125	30,478,228	275,590	368,125	344,719	341,170	407,598	357,052
Scotland	152	163	131	2,041,129	1,915,398	1,397,546	21,624	30,110	31,864	34,698	41,237	39,809
Ireland	12	9	13	150,512	119,944	124,240	1,633	1,757	2,746	3,345	2,734	4,203
United Kingdom .	2,210	2,887	2,549	28,010,217	30,387,467	32,000,014	298,847	399,992	379,329	379,213	451,569	401,064
WOOLLEN, WORSTED AND SHODDY FACTORIES:												
England and Wales	1,793	1,968	2,211	2,798,275	3,092,376	6,045,049	52,535	63,312	115,122	155,820	159,281	233,535
Scotland	204	201	207	293,362	356,131	385,246	800	1,383	3,528	10,175	12,728	18,174
Ireland	33	42	47	19,884	23,274	25,584	64	123	215	890	1,037	*1,347
United Kingdom .	2,030	2,211	2,465	3,111,521	3,471,781	6,455,879	53,399	64,818	118,865	166,885	173,046	253,056
FLAX, HEMP, AND JUTE FACTORIES:												
England and Wales	139	143	155	441,759	345,192	448,909	1,987	2,161	5,530	19,787	20,474	24,949
Scotland	168	192	169	278,304	312,239	331,151	5,011	8,520	15,828	31,722	39,562	52,639
Ireland	110	105	148	567,980	594,805	899,297	1,691	4,666	13,689	28,753	33,967	57,745
United Kingdom .	417	440	472	1,288,043	1,252,236	1,679,357	8,689	15,347	35,047	80,262	94,003	135,333

* As given in the return for 1868, the number of persons employed in the Woollen, &c., manufacture in Ireland is 10,555. This is an obvious error, and I have corrected it by estimating the number of persons employed, on the basis of the number of spindles and looms given in the return.

Mr. G. R. Porter, in his "Progress of the Nation" gives a statement from the books of Mr. Thomas Houldsworth, laid before the Committee on Manufactures, which sat in

Illustration of effect of improvement of machinery from the

CHAP. V.

"Progress of the Nation."

1833; and he shows in a similar manner the powers of machinery in augmenting the productive powers, as well as the earnings of the operative :—

Year.	Work turned off by one Spinner per week		Wages per week				Prices from Greenwich Hospital Records		Quantities which a week's nett earnings would purchase	
	lbs.	Nos.	Gross	Piecers	Nett	Hours of work per week	Flour per sack	Flesh per lb.	Lbs. of Flour	Lbs. of Flesh
			s. d.	s. d.	s. d.		s. d.	d. d.		
1804	12	180	60 0	27 6	32 6	74	83 0	6 to 7	117	62½
,,	9	200	67 6	31 0	36 6	74	83 0	6 to 7	124	73
'14	18	180	72 0	27 6	44 6	74	70 6	8	175	67
	13½	200	90 0	30 0	60 0	74	70 6	8	239	90
1833	22½	180	54 8	21 0	33 8	69	45 0	6	210	67
,,	19	200	65 3	22 6	42 9	69	45 0	6	267	85

The development of the productive power of machinery by increasing the proportion of spindles to the number of hands employed is not a novelty of our time. Mr. Porter's work contains the following interesting calculation of the results attained by a former generation of cotton spinners :—

Spinners' wages.

"In the cotton-mill of Messrs. Houldsworths in Glasgow, a spinner employed on a mule of 3,360 spindles and spinning cotton 120 hanks to the pound, produced, in 1823, working 74½ hours in the week, 46 pounds of yarn, his nett weekly earnings for which amounted to 26*s.* 7*d.* In 1833, the rate of wages having in the meanwhile been reduced 13⅓ per cent., and the time of working having been lessened to 69 hours, the spinner was enabled by the greater perfection of the machinery, to produce, on a mule of the same number of spindles, 52½ pounds of yarn of the same fineness, and his nett weekly earnings were advanced to 29*s.* 10*d.*"

Mr. Cowell s evidence.

But a much more considerable economy than this was produced by increasing the size of the mules. Mr. Cowell, in the Supplementary Report of the Factory Commissioners, gives the following example of the effect on the spinner's earnings :—" In the early part of last year a spinner produced 16 pounds of yarn of No. 200 from mules of the power of 300 to 324 spindles. Consulting the list of prices, I perceive that in May he was paid 3*s.* 6*d.* a pound : this gives 54*s.* for his gross receipts, out of which he had to pay 13*s.* for assistants. This leaves him with 41*s.* earnings. His mules are now converted into mules of the power of 648 ; he is paid 2*s.* 5*d.*

CHAP. V.

a pound instead of 3*s.* 6*d.*; but he produces 32 pounds of yarn of the fineness of 200 hanks to the pound in 69 hours. His gross receipts are immediately raised to 77*s.* 4*d.* He requires five assistants to help him; but deducting 27*s.* for their pay from his gross receipts, there remains a sum of 50*s.* 4*d.* for his nett earnings for 69 hours' work, instead of 41*s.*, an increase of more than 20 per cent., while the cost of the yarn is reduced 13*d.* per pound."

The cost of making railways reduced by improved systems of working and mechanical appliances. Mr. Rowan.

It is perhaps less easy to substitute machinery for manual labour in engineering work than in any other branch of industry. But even in the construction of railways, labour has been greatly economised.

In Denmark the cost of constructing railways has been reduced by 35 per cent. This reduction is entirely due to the improved system of working introduced by Mr. Rowan, the engineer, who has represented the firm of Peto, Brassey, and Betts, in their Danish contracts.

Mr. Ballard.

Mr. Ballard, who has had great experience in making railways in England, gives a similar explanation of the reduction in the cost of making railways. He says that in England, as abroad, contractors can now obtain the co-operation of much more experienced sub-contractors; and that the introduction of the locomotive has made it practicable to carry a load of earth to a greater distance for the same money.

Mr. Wilcox.

Mr. Wilcox, who has executed important contracts in Australia, in reply to the question as to whether it costs more to make a railway now than it did twenty years ago, replies :—"I am of opinion that railways are now made considerably cheaper, though the rate paid for labour has increased to the extent perhaps of fifteen or twenty per cent. Railways are now less costly, owing to the greater skill in construction, and from other appliances being so much employed to do work which was formerly performed only by the labour of men and horses."

Mr. Nasmyth on the increase of machinery

Mr. Nasmyth, in his evidence before the Trades Unions Commissioners, described very graphically how the long strike of 1851 made him anxious to develop to the utmost the use

CHAP. V.

after the strike of 1851.

of labour-saving machinery. "The great feature," he said, "of our modern mechanical improvement has been the introduction of self-acting tools. All that a mechanic has to do, and which any lad is able to do, is, not to labour, but to watch the beautiful functions of the machine. All that class of men, who depended upon mere dexterity, are set aside altogether. I had four boys to one mechanic, By these mechanical contrivances I reduced the number of men in my employ 1,500 hands, fully one half. The result was that my profits were much increased."

Other examples of reduction of cost by the use of machinery.

With the increased use of machinery labourers can now be employed to make parts of locomotives which formerly could only have been produced by skilled artisans. By these means, in one of the largest locomotive establishments in England, the cost of manufacturing a first-class engine and tender has been steadily diminished, and the re-manufacture of iron rails which, in 1860, cost 7*l.* 15*s.* 0*d.* per ton, was reduced in eight years to 7*l.* 0*s.* 2*d.* per ton. In both cases the old rails were charged at the same price per ton.

Mr. Manby's experience.

In the opinion of Mr. Charles Manby, the price of locomotives is 7½ per cent. less than it was, having been reduced on the average, say from 2,600*l.* to 2,300*l.* There have been no changes in the rate of wages; but production is cheaper through the application of improved machinery.

Mr. Lothian Bell on the improvement of furnaces in consequence of the high price of fuel.

Formerly, the furnaces in use in our iron manufacture were constructed with little regard to economy of fuel; but Mr. Lothian Bell says that, as soon as the cost of fuel increased, our manufacturers adopted the best methods for the purification of the coal, and for its conversion into coke, for the use of waste heat from furnaces in driving machinery and for the use of the best furnace gases, and that 500,000 tons of coal are annually saved by these discoveries in the Cleveland district alone.

Mr. Buddicom on economy of fuel in France.

Mr. Buddicom, an English locomotive engineer, who has had thirty years' experience on the Continent, and who was at the head of the Sotteville Works, a large establishment near Rouen, explains how the special difficulties with which they had to

CHAP. V.

contend, have stimulated the ingenuity of French engineers: "Formerly, when I was actively engaged in locomotive building, greater study was given to save the consumption of fuel in the workshops in France than in England. Fuel was so expensive, it cost 25*s*. a ton, that before the drawings of any piece of machinery were completed, the question of the quantity of fuel necessary to be used in producing it was a consideration, and frequently the form or the method of construction originally proposed, underwent an entire modification, with a view to economize coal. I know that at one time my consumption of fuel for the manufacture of an engine did not exceed the cost of the fuel consumed in England; although the price of fuel in England was about one-third of the amount which we had to pay."

Mr. Hodges on labour-saving processes and appliances in the United States.

The following extracts from the evidence of Mr. Hodges, who has had great experience in America, supply further illustrations of the stimulus given to the inventive faculty, by the difficulty arising from the high price of labour and the dearness of raw materials.

"In America the leading wheels of the locomotives and all the wheels of the railway carriages are constructed of cast-iron ; but the railway authorities of this country would not sanction the use of cast-iron for those purposes. It is doubtful, indeed, whether cast-iron wheels could be obtained in this country of such quality as to endure the wear and tear of railway traffic. In America cast-iron wheels are made of chilled iron, and they are found to answer the purpose admirably. At the commencement of the Grand Trunk Railway of Canada, a large quantity of cast-iron wheels were sent out from England, but it was found that they did not last. Wrought-iron wheels were then tried ; but even these would not stand the work for which they were designed."

American climate.

"In America the climate presents peculiar difficulties. When the summer weather breaks up there is a month of continuous rain, followed by intensely severe frost. The effect of the changes of weather was to consolidate the sleepers upon which the rails were placed, and to convert the ballast into

V.

an intensely hard mass, as rigid as the solid rock. When trains pass over a railway in this condition. a very severe jar is necessarily experienced causing exceptional wear and tear to the rolling stock. The Americans have been able to construct wheels of cast-iron, which will stand this; while we in England have scarcely been able to produce, even in wrought-iron, wheels which will endure the strain to which they are subjected in America. Again, Americans have displayed marvellous energy in the construction of all light machinery."

Ironwork.

"The United States ironmasters have made wonderful strides, and their axles are amazingly strong, they are better than English axles. There is now a large manufactory at Montreal for axles, and their castings are admirable. Take, for example, such simple things as rain-water pipes. They are beautifully cast. You see them scarcely more than the eighth of an inch thick. We should have them five times as thick."

"In cast-iron they beat us out of the market. The superior quality of their cast-iron is due to their great skill in mixing the ores. The extreme cost of labour is the reason why they make these things of cast-iron."

"The construction of rolling stock formed a part of the contract for the Grand Trunk Railway, and when the contractors were about to establish workshops for the purpose of constructing carriages and other rolling stock, two clever mechanics were sent through the United States to examine the principal establishments in which similar railway stock was constructed. Although these men represented, as it were, a competition in trade, they were extremely well received wherever they went. They were freely supplied with drawings of all the most successful machines, and with every information necessary to enable them to set up similar apparatus. Every well tried labour-saving machine was introduced into our workshops. In England, in 1853, there were no morticing machines, and no planing machines such as we now see in every well-furnished establishment; but they had all

CHAP. V.

those machines in Canada supplied from American manufacturers."

Mr. Hodges, while speaking in commendatory terms of the ingenuity displayed by the Americans in the contrivance of all light machinery, is of opinion that in the construction of machinery for undertaking heavy work, England has carried the palm against every other nation.

Mr. Field on labour-saving machinery in the hardware manufacture in the United States.

Mr. Alfred Field told the Committee on Scientific Education that, in the United States, a workman in the hardware trade earns double the daily wages of an English workman; but labour-saving appliances have been brought to such perfection that in twenty-five classes of hardware goods, the United States are able to export largely into countries in which the pay of artisans is scarcely a quarter of the wage paid in America. They send their spades, shovels, axes, coopers' tools, and pumps to England; although raw material and wages are twice as dear in the United States as in England.

The rates of wages ordered for farm-labourers at the Labour Exchange in San

CHAP. V.

Francisco, in September 1870, were during the winter season from 5*l.* to 6*l.* per month and food and lodging found, and from 8*l.* to 9*l.* and food and lodging found, during harvest. The wages of operatives in California were still more in advance of the rates paid in other States of the Union. Observe the effect of these extreme prices for labour. "The number of farm labourers required in this state," says Mr. Booker, "is less in proportion to the land cultivated than in any other part of the Union. It probably does not exceed one hand to 100 acres. Every agricultural operation is performed by machinery. A great deal of soil is light, permitting the use of gang ploughs, and on the lightest lands the seed is distributed by the plough in front of the shares. Nothing more is done until the grain is ready for the sickle, when the reaping machine is used, and the threshing machine follows it."

High agricultural wages in California have led to the increased use of machinery.

The recently published Blue Book on the tenure of land in foreign countries is a compilation of immense value, and does honour to the diplomatic service of this country. It

The use of machinery and cost of labour in Russia and California compared.

CHAP. V.

contains most interesting illustrations of the laws which govern the labour question. I have already, by numerous examples, endeavoured to show that where labour is cheapest, the indifference to labour-saving machinery is most conspicuous; and that where labour is dearest it is most effectually economised. These axioms are strikingly illustrated by a comparison of the agriculture of Russia and Prussia with the agriculture of the United States and of those European countries in which labour is most liberally paid. To give a single example of this contrast of labourers to land in Russia, the proportion is one man to every 11½ acres. In Pennsylvania two men by the year, with two others during the harvest, will do the whole of the work on a farm of 100 acres.

Labour-saving machinery in United States.

In the United States the application of labour-saving machinery to agricultural operations is increasing every year. The number of patents issued for agricultural implements was, in 1847, 43; in 1863, 390; in 1864, 563; in 1866, 1,778; and in 1867, 1,800.

A few years ago Mr. McCormack, at

Chicago, had already made 80,000 reaping machines.

In spite of the great difference in the rate of wages in favour of the continental producers, Messrs. Ransom and Sims are, and have long been exporting agricultural implements on a large scale to Russia, Japan, China, Hungary, Austria and Turkey.

Though in articles of iron we enjoy a pre-eminence over the rest of the world, in machines in which wood is more used the Americans compete with England successfully. They export a large number of reaping machines to Austria and to England. Wood's grass mower, an American machine, is much used in this country, and their horse-power machines are generally much cheaper than ours. They have an advantage in an abundant supply of cheap wood. But their skill in contriving machines for the purpose of working up wood into articles useful for men has enabled them to overcome the difficulties of high priced labour in competition with other countries in which much lower rates of wages prevail.

CHAP. V.

The rise in agricultural wages and in rents in England has led to an increase of machinery.

In English agriculture the rise of wages has been considerable. It was recently stated by Mr. C. S. Read, M.P., that "within the last twenty years the remuneration of agricultural labourers had increased about 35 per cent. In 1851, in the six counties in which agricultural wages are the lowest, the average was 7*s.* 1½*d.* per week. The wages in Dorsetshire, where the lowest rate is still paid, are now 8*s.* In the Cotswold they range from 10*s.* to 14*s.*, and in Northumberland from 13*s.* to 15*s.* Farmers on light arable soils pay a higher rent per acre than they did twenty years ago. Then they paid 25*s.*, now it costs them 35*s.*, he did not get off under 40*s.*"

I have quoted numerous examples to show how much dear labour stimulates invention, and how indifferent men become to the value of mechanical appliance when manual labour is very cheap.

As an amusing instance of the incapacity of unskilful men in its most exaggerated form, I may mention a case which occurred in Jamaica, on the only railway which has been executed in that island. The usual plant required for the construction of the railway had been sent out, and the native labourers were supplied with barrows for the purpose of removing the earth. When these men began to work they were so ignorant of the mechanical advantages to be derived from the use of the barrow, that they placed these vehicles, laden with earth, upon the top of their heads: and it was not without much expostulation that the English foremen were enabled to induce them to try the effect of placing the barrow on a plank, and wheeling instead of carrying the load.

It is by improved methods of husbandry, and by superior machinery alone, that agriculturists are enabled to pay higher wages and higher rents and yet obtain a moderate return on their capital, and some remuneration for their scientific education and personal attention to their business.

An examination of these remarkable illustrations of the ingenuity of man, when his powers are developed by difficulties, confirms the opinion already expressed that the productive powers of the different nations are

CHAP. V. more equal than might have been expected. Dear labour is the great obstacle to the extension of British trade. But we see how the cheap labour at the command of our competitors seems to exercise the same enervating influence as the delights of Capua on the soldiers of Hannibal.

CHAPTER VI.

HOURS OF LABOUR.

The number of hours per day no measure of the amount of work.

I HAVE said that the mere rate of daily wages affords no indication of the cost of executing work. It is equally true that the hours of labour are no criterion of the amount of work performed. In 1842 Messrs. Hornby, at Blackburn, made a calculation that even if their operatives were paid the same sum for working sixty as for working sixty-nine hours per week, the increased cost would be so small, as not to be weighed in the balance against the advantage to the operatives themselves of a larger amount of leisure. More recently, MM. Dollfus of Mulhausen reduced the working hours of their establishment from twelve hours to eleven hours per day, and promised the men that no reduction should

MM. Dollfus.

CHAP. VI.

be made in their wages, if they performed the same quantity of work. After a month had elapsed it was found that the men did, in eleven hours, not only as much work but five per cent. more than they had previously performed in a day of twelve hours.

South Wales.

Miners work on the average twelve hours a day in South Wales and only seven hours in the north of England; and yet Mr. G. Elliott, M.P., has found that the cost of getting coals in Aberdare is twenty-five per cent. more than it is in Northumberland.

Russia.

"In Russia, the peasantry begin to work in summer," says Mr. Michell, "at 2 A.M., when working for themselves, and finish at 9 P.M., with periods of rest equal to two or three hours, leaving from sixteen to seventeen hours' work per day. Persons competent to form an opinion consider that an English farm labourer would do the work of two Russian labourers—the latter working sixteen and the former only ten hours."

In the foregoing case greater diligence, when at work, has enabled the energetic and laborious Englishman, to do more work in a shorter time than the Russian peasant, with whom he has been compared. Unless there be this superior vigour and industry, a reduction of hours is only an increase of wages in another form. It is possible that the workman may be justified in demanding such an increase; and assuming that the profits of trade do justify a rise of wages, there cannot be a more legitimate mode of raising wages than by reducing the working hours. But it must be remembered that trades, which can only flourish by successful competition with the foreigner, must, to a certain extent, be regulated with reference to rules established abroad.

The English workmen must not allow the cost of labour in England to exceed the cost abroad.

In the United States the usual hours of labour are ten hours a day. In Germany, France, and on the Continent generally, the working hours are longer than with us. The British workman must take care that he does not, by working shorter hours, so increase the cost of production, that competition with foreign industry becomes impossible.

A reduction in the hours of labour does not necessarily involve a corresponding reduction of work performed. A little more diligence will easily enable a workman to get through as much work in nine hours as in ten hours.

On railways many opportunities have occurred of ascertaining to what extent the amount of work executed in a day, is regulated by an extension or a reduction in the hours of labour. On the Paris and Rouen line, the Frenchmen were in the habit of coming to work in the summer at five in the morning, and they left off at seven in the evening. The Englishmen never came to work before six, and always left off at half-past-five: but the amount of work executed by the Englishmen in the shorter time was much greater than the amount of work executed by the Frenchmen, notwithstanding the longer hours in which they laboured.

During the construction of the Trent Valley line, immense efforts were made to complete the work in the shortest possible time, and in order to expedite to the utmost degree the completion of the station at

Atherstone, two shifts of men were employed on the building, each of them working eight hours a day. It was found that each shift, although working for only eight hours did more work in a day than other men employed for the full number of hours which at that time constituted a day's work, viz. ten hours per day.

A very recent illustration of the increased diligence with which men are wont to labour when their hours of work are reduced, has been brought to my knowledge by Mr. Biddle, the manager of the large establishment of Messrs. Ransome and Sims at Ipswich, in which 1,200 artisans are employed.

On January 2 of the present year, the hours of work were reduced from 58½ hours to 54 hours a week. But the men working the engineer's tools have so successfully striven to protect themselves against the risk of diminution of wages from the nine hours' movement when employed in doing piece work, that the power required to work

CHAP. VI.

the tools has actually been increased from twelve to fifteen per cent.

With regard to vice work, all of which is done by hand, the operatives execute quite as much as in the previous longer hours.

In the blacksmiths' shop, where there is a great variety of work, the men are in every case making equally good wages on the old piece-work prices. The same remark applies to the iron moulders.

Solution of the difficulty in relays of mechanics.

Turning from these significant facts to the general question of the combination of human labour with machine power, it will not be denied that it is impossible for the human machine to keep pace with machinery made of brass and iron. But why should not a machine, which never tires, be tended by two or three artisans, relieving each other, as one watch relieves another on board ship? In driving the machinery of steam ships it has been found necessary, on all long voyages, to have three sets of engineers and firemen. Why should not the day be divided into three periods of eight hours, or the working day be extended to sixteen hours—two sets of men being employed? The change arising from the increasing use of machinery seems to render corresponding modifications in the application of labour to industrial production essential.

Mr. Alexander on "Relays."

I am aware that my solution of the difficulty is not universally, nor perhaps generally, approved by practical men. The following remarks by Mr. Alexander, whose name has been already mentioned, very forcibly and clearly set forth the arguments of those who are opposed to a change in the present system. "With reference to increasing the productive power of plant by working it on the 'relay' system, there are two suggestions, which may be offered in support of the idea that such a scheme will not prove so remunerative as might be anticipated. In the first place, it is unnatural. It is true that our systems have changed greatly since the 'good old times' when we were told that 'the night cometh when no man can work.' But still the fact remains that up till now men love the daylight rather than darkness, and moreover require (a fact to be noted by

CHAP. VI.

the political economist) considerably increased wages when on night shifts than when on day duty."

Extra wages on "night shifts."

"The amount varies from twenty-five to fifty per cent. in excess of the ordinary wages. A very serious addition; and this must therefore be set against any advantage gained by the more continuous application of fixed capital to the powers of machinery. Again, I have found practically that the system is not conducive to economical maintenance of machinery. A good workman comes to like—shall I say love—the machine which seems to share his labour. A workman in comfortable circumstances—and no true workman should be otherwise—learns to appreciate the merits of the machine entrusted to his care; and I have heard him bewail the short-sighted policy of its owner who stinted it in needful repairs, or insisted on administering cheaper and inferior oil, with the same kind of pathetic sorrow with which we may hear a mother regretting her inability to procure suitable medicine for an ailing child. Now this kindly and excellent feeling, based on admiration and support to something dependent, is completely broken down by handing over special machines to the care of several people. No doubt it has been and must be done in certain cases. On the Metropolitan and North London Railways, for instance, where 'omnibus' trains run at short intervals continued for a number of hours, no other plan so economical could probably be adopted. But I speak from experience when I say, generally, that engineering machines entrusted to different workmen are not nearly so well kept as when each has his machine under his peculiar care, and that 'break-downs' and damage are much more frequent. Indeed, unless there be a minute inspection at each change, which is nearly impracticable in a large establishment, it becomes very difficult to fix the responsibility for the deterioration which occurs upon anyone in particular." I know my correspondent to be a practical man, and I am moved by the eloquence of his appeal; but in deciding these disputed questions impartiality is essential, in order to

Omnibus trains.

form a sound opinion; and I am therefore disposed to adhere to my own suggestion in favour of the system of relays of mechanics to tend machinery. There are difficulties in every system, but the relay system seems the best way of applying the exhaustible powers of man to the inexhaustible machine.

M. Jules Simon on Labour.

The leisure which they enjoy is the highest privilege of the wealthy. The want of opportunity for thought and cultivation is the greatest privation of those who are compelled to pass the greater portion of their lives in manual or in mental toil. In the eloquent language of M. Jules Simon, in his essay on Labour: "Cette condition paraît assez dure. Ce n'est pas à cause du travail, dont personne ne se plaint, ni à cause de la privation du superflu; c'est parce que dans une vie ainsi faite il ne reste pas de place pour l'étude, pour la possession de soi-même. Ce besoin d'étudier et de penser n'existe pas partout, même en France. Il faut pour l'éprouver une certaine élévation de sentiment, autrefois rare, aujourd'hui presque universelle, au moins dans les grands centres de population. A quoi tient ce changement? Au progrès général, aux merveilles scientifiques accomplies chaque jour sous les yeux de la foule, à l'augmentation de bien-être résultant de l'augmentation du nombre des produits manufacturés, à une instruction plus étendue et plus répandue, à l'orgueil légitime inspiré par les souvenirs de la Révolution et par la possession des droits politiques."

The demand for a larger share in the intellectual enjoyments of life is a necessary result of the diffusion of education among the masses of the people. But the workmen must recognise the necessity of developing to the utmost their energy and their skill, in order to justify a demand for diminished hours of labour in an industry in which the profits of the employers are already so moderate that they cannot be further reduced without altogether preventing the investment of the capital in the business.

CHAPTER VII.

RISE OF WAGES ABROAD.

CHAP. VII.

Have wages risen more rapidly in England than in other countries?

I WILL next proceed to examine the statements, widely circulated and largely accepted by the public, to the effect that there has been a greater advance in the wages of operatives in recent years in England, than in the corresponding period abroad. If it were true that the workmen in union possessed a great power which they could not exercise without the aid of their trade combinations, the development of these societies would become a question of the utmost gravity to the commercial interests of the country. I have, therefore, thought it most important to ascertain how far the statements which have gained credence are justified by facts. For the purpose of elucidating this portion of the subject under discussion, I have obtained tabulative statements extending over the last sixteen years, and showing the comparative rate of wages in several important manufacturing establishments in this country, in which many of the workmen employed belonged to the much dreaded Trades Unions. Full and accurate information on the actual rate and progressive increase of wages abroad, where Trades Unions until very recently did not exist, is contained in the valuable Reports on these subjects which were specially made to Lord Stanley by the Secretaries of Embassy and Legation. I will begin by stating how the case stands as regards the engineering trade in England. In this trade since 1852, there has been no augmentation until quite recently in the wages earned by the operatives. The reason is obvious. The rate of wages in England is limited by the necessity of competition with the foreign manufacturers. Employers in England, as elsewhere, only employ labour on the assumption that they

Wages of mechanics in England.

can realize a profit by their business; and in the engineering trade, in consequence of the impossibility of increasing the cost of production without losing our trade in the neutral markets, it has not until lately been possible to make an advance of wages. On the other hand, the active competition between the numerous body of manufacturers in the country has reduced profits to a rate so moderate that, if it were to be further reduced, the trade would no longer offer any inducement for the investment of capital. I give in a tabular form a statement of the wages at the Canada Works at Birkenhead, since the formation of that establishment.

Wages at the Canada Works.

The average number of hands on the books is 600; a sufficient number to afford a fair opportunity of testing the average wages in the mechanical trades throughout the country. It will be seen, on examination of the table, that there has been no appreciable improvement in the rates of pay in recent years.

Average Rates of Wages Paid to Skilled Workmen at the Canada Works, Birkenhead.

	1854	1855	1856	1857	1858	1859	1860	1861	1862	1863	1864	1865	1866	1867	1868	1869
	s. d.	*s. d.*	*s. d.*	*s. d.*	*s. d.*	*s. d.*	*s. d.*	*s. d.*	*s. d.*	*s. d.*	*s. d.*	*s. d.*	*s. d.*	*s. d.*	*s. d.*	*s. d.*
Fitters . . .	29 0	28 3	29 0	30 6	28 10	27 6	27 6	27 0	27 10	28 0	28 0	28 1	31 0	32 6	31 0	30 0
Turners . . .	29 4	30 3	31 3	33 0	31 6	31 0	32 0	31 6	32 0	31 6	31 6	31 5	31 6	31 0	30 0	29 4
Coppersmiths and Braziers	31 6	30 10	28 10	29 0	28 0	30 0	31 0	29 6	28 6	28 1	31 6	31 7	32 6	32 0	32 0	30 9
Grinders . . .	27 0	27 0	27 0	24 0	24 0	22 0	26 0	25 6	27 0	27 6	27 6	32 0	28 6	32 0	26 6	23 0
Smiths . . .	31 0	31 5	32 0	31 0	30 0	29 6	30 3	30 0	29 6	31 0	30 6	30 3	31 9	32 9	31 6	30 0
Boiler Smiths .	34 0	34 0	35 0	34 0	32 6	33 0	33 8	33 0	32 6	33 0	33 0	34 6	36 0	37 0	36 0	36 0
Bricklayers . .	34 0	34 0	34 0	34 0	34 0	34 0	34 0	34 0	34 0	34 0	34 0	34 0	34 0	34 0	34 0	34 0
Saddlers and Belt Makers	26 0	27 0	26 0	26 0	27 0	26 0	27 0	27 0	27 0	27 0	27 0	25 6	24 0	24 0	25 0	26 0
Forgemen . .	36 6	37 0	36 0	33 6	—	—	33 0	36 0	35 6	35 0	34 6	33 0	32 9	33 0	32 6	32 6
Painters . . .	24 0	23 0	24 0	26 0	26 6	25 0	27 0	26 0	25 6	25 6	25 8	26 6	27 6	24 6	24 0	23 0
Moulders . .	32 0	31 6	33 0	33 0	32 0	31 6	31 6	32 6	32 0	32 6	33 0	33 0	32 9	34 6	34 2	31 6
Joiners and Pattern Makers	28 0	28 6	29 0	28 2	27 6	29 0	29 6	30 0	29 6	29 6	29 0	30 0	30 6	31 4	30 9	30 0
Boiler Makers .	31 6	31 0	30 6	32 6	2 0	30 6	31 0	31 6	31 0	31 6	31 3	31 9	34 2	3 0	32 0	32 0

Again, the experience of the same establishment is equally conclusive in proof of the opinion that the rate of wages is regulated of necessity by the ratio between the supply of labour and the demand; and that when the supply exceeds the demand, wages must inevitably fall, if the depression in trade is long protracted. During the contraction of trade consequent upon the late financial crisis, the price of piece-work had been reduced at the Canada Works sufficiently to allow of the construction of locomotives and bridge work at a cheaper rate than at any

CHAP. VII.

Supply and demand.

CHAP. VII.

time during the last fifteen years; thus fully confirming the opinion that Trades Unions can never succeed in advancing wages, except when the prospects of trade are favourable.

Wages on the Continent have risen more rapidly than in England.

On the other hand, the advanced rate of wages abroad proves that, through the development of manufacturing industry, the wages of the working classes have risen more rapidly than in any branch of industry in this country. The rise of wages abroad is mainly caused by increased demand for labour; but it is partly due to the augmented cost of living.

Partly in consequence of the greater rise of prices.

Mr. Fane.

In France, Belgium, and Prussia, the three great competing countries with England, prices are from twenty to thirty per cent. dearer than twenty years ago; and this increase in the cost of living tells immediately upon the price of all labour, especially of common or unskilled labour. In France, twenty years ago, labourers were content to work for 1*s.* 6*d.* a day. At the present time, from 2*s.* 2*d.* to 2*s.* 4*d.* is the ordinary rate of pay. Mr. Fane says, in his report to Lord Stanley, that "the general rate of money wages in France has increased about forty per cent. in the last fifteen years, in those industries which compete with foreigners in the neutral markets. This rise in the money wages has been accompanied by a considerable rise in the price of food and clothing; still, the relative proportions in which money wages and the price of commodities have risen, leave a margin in favour of the former."

Increase of manufactures has raised agricultural wages. Mr. Wells.

Mr. Wells attributes the rise in the price of agricultural labour in France and Germany to the drain which is constantly taking place from the rural districts into the towns. The increase of manufacturing industry has caused much embarrassment to agriculture, and a further supply of labour from the same source can only be obtained by the payment of higher wages.

There cannot be a doubt that the same observation is equally applicable to Warwickshire at the present time.

Rise of Wages at Creuzot.

In the famous engine building establishment at Creuzot, founded by the father of Mr. Charles Manby, 10,000 persons are now employed, and the annual expenditure in

CHAP. VII.

wages amounts to 400,000*l.* Mechanics were paid, when the establishment was first created, at the rate of 2½ francs a day. At the present time none receive less than 5 francs a day. Between 1850 and 1866, the mean rate advanced from 2*s.* to 2*s.* 11*d.* per head, or thirty-eight per cent., and some men earned from 6*s.* 8*d.* to 8*s.* 4*d.* per day. In addition to their money wages, great facilities are given to the workpeople, at the expense of the proprietors, for feeding, clothing, and educating themselves and their families: 700 families of the operatives are lodged by the company at fifty per cent. below the normal rate of house rent, and 700 gardens are let at the nominal rent of 2 francs per annum. Compare what has occurred in this country with what has taken place at MM. Schneider's, at Creuzot, and it will be clearly proved, as I think, how small is the power of a Trades Union in comparison with the natural effects of an increasing trade and increasing competition among masters for the supply of labour. At MM. Schneider's, without the assistance of a Trades Union, the working people have obtained, during the last seventeen years, an augmentation of wage of thirty-eight per cent. In England, in the corresponding period, the most powerful of all the Trade Societies, with an accumulated fund of 149,000*l.*, has found it impossible to secure any increase in the earnings of its members.

Wages of tailors in Paris—M. Dusantoy.

I shall next refer to the case of the tailoring trades. At the military clothing establishment of M. Dusautoy, in Paris, there are 3,300 persons employed, 800 of them being men, 2,000 women, and 500 children. The amount of wages paid in 1866 amounted to 100,000*l.* in the year. The daily wages for men ranged from 3*s.* 4*d.* to 8*s.* 4*d.*; while in London the rate is stated by Professor Levi, in his essay on the wages and earnings of the working classes, to be from 4*s.* to 7*s.* At M. Dusautoy's, women earn from 2½ to 4 francs a day. In London the wages of girls are 1*s.*, and of women employed as seamstresses from 2*s.* to 2*s.* 6*d.* a day. The children at M. Dusautoy's earn from 1 to 2 francs a day. In London their wages would be about 1*s.*

CHAP. VII.

Rise in wages of machine-tool makers.

In France machine tools are made to the value of 2,000,000 of francs annually; but, though the raw materials used are much cheaper since the negotiation of the Treaty of Commerce with this country, the selling price continues the same, owing to the increasing dearness of labour.

Rise of wages in Italy;

In Italy since 1861 wages have risen considerably, in some trades to the extent of thirty to fifty per cent. It has been stated that in Sicily, since 1860, the pay of the working classes has doubled. A field labourer in that island now earns from 1*s.* 4*d.* to 2*s.* 8*d.* a day. In Lower Silesia the rates of wages have doubled generally within the memory of the older workmen. At the great zinc works known as the Vielle Montagne near Liège, where 6,500 hands are employed, in twelve years the wages have increased forty-five per cent. It is therefore clear that the difficulties of the labour question are likely to be felt quite as severely on the Continent as in this country, and that they will hereafter increase in proportion to the increase of continental production.

in Belgium.

The rise in England would have been greater without free trade.

Wages in England would have risen to a far higher scale than has hitherto been reached; unless the enlightened policy of free trade had been adopted, and the improved communications both by sea and land had given increased facilities for the importation of cattle and other supplies from distant countries. A perusal of the following statement of the prices of provisions in the rural districts of Staffordshire will show how much has been accomplished by our liberal fiscal policy in reducing the cost of the necessaries of life.

A rise of wages in London inevitable.

The question of rent is inferior only in its importance to the domestic economy of the working man to the price of food. Owing to the great rise in rents and the increased burdens of taxation in London during the last twenty years, an advance of wages was inevitable. The working classes have been subjected to most serious inconvenience by the demolition of whole suburbs by railway companies.

In a debate in the House of Lords on the Artisans and Labourers Dwellings Bill, Lord Chelmsford said that the poorer descriptions

Statement of Prices of Provisions (Retail) extracted from the Books

	1849	1850	1851	1852	1853	1854	1855	1856	1857	1858
	£ s. d.	£ s. d.	£ s. d.	£ s. d.	£ s. d.	£ s. d.	£ s. d.	£ s. d.	£ s. d.	£ s. d.
Flour per sack	1 11 6	1 7 0	1 8 0	1 10 0	1 15 6	2 2 6	2 5 0	2 2 6	1 18 6	1 10 6
Cheese per lb.	0 0 6½	0 0 6½	0 0 6½	0 0 6	0 0 6½	0 0 7	0 0 7	0 0 8	0 0 9	0 0 8
Butter ditto .	0 1 2	0 1 3	0 1 1	0 1 2	0 1 2	0 1 4	0 1 4	0 1 4	0 1 4	0 1 4
Bacon ditto .	0 0 8	0 0 7½	0 0 8	0 0 7½	0 0 8	0 0 7	0 0 8	0 0 8½	0 0 9	0 0 8
Tea ditto . .	0 5 0	0 5 0	0 5 0	0 5 0	0 5 0	0 5 0	0 5 0	0 5 0	0 5 0	0 4 8
Coffee ditto .	0 1 6	0 1 6	0 1 4	0 1 4	0 1 4	0 1 4	0 1 4	0 1 4	0 1 4	0 1 4
Sugar ditto .	0 0 5¼	0 0 5¼	0 0 5	0 0 5	0 0 5	0 0 5	0 0 5	0 0 5	0 0 6½	0 0 6
Candles ditto .	0 0 6	0 0 5¼	0 0 5¼	0 0 5	0 0 6¼	0 0 7½	0 0 7¼	0 0 7¼	0 0 7½	0 0 7
Soap ditto . .	0 0 5¼	0 0 6	0 0 5¼	0 0 5¼	0 0 5	0 0 5	0 0 5	0 0 4½	0 0 4½	0 0 4½
Beef ditto . .	0 0 7	0 0 6	0 0 6	0 0 6	0 0 7	0 0 7	0 0 7½	0 0 7½	0 0 7½	0 0 7½
Mutton ditto .	0 0 6½	0 0 6	0 0 6	0 0 6	0 0 7	0 0 7	0 0 7½	0 0 7½	0 0 7½	0 0 7
Bread ditto .	0 0 1½	0 0 1⅛	0 0 1¼	0 0 1¼	0 0 1½	0 0 2⅛	0 0 2¼	0 0 2⅛	0 0 1⅝	0 0 1¼

CHAP. VII.

of property in London were daily increasing in value, and he referred, among other evidence, to the report of the Rev. Mr. Andrews, Incumbent of St. Luke's, King's Cross, in which it was stated that the Midland Company had demolished 275 houses in his parish, and that the population had been reduced from 8,050 to 3,800. In Old St. Pancras 750 houses had been pulled down and 1,800 persons ejected. The rents in that neighbourhood had risen in consequence twenty per cent. On the site selected for the Law Courts 206 houses, containing 1,120 families, had been demolished.

St. Pancras.

Law Courts.

Sir Sydney Waterlow.

I am informed by Sir Sydney Waterlow, that in London, working men, earning from *of Mr. George Dix, Grocer and General Dealer, May* 26, 1869.

1859			1860			1861			1862			1863			1864			1865			1866			1867			1868			1869		
£	*s.*	*d.*	£	*s.*	*d.*	£	*s.*	*d.*	£	*s.*	*d.*	£	*s.*	*d.*	£	*s.*	*d.*	£	*s.*	*d.*	£	*s.*	*d.*	£	*s.*	*d.*	£	*s.*	*d.*	£	*s.*	*d.*
1	9	6	1	14	0	1	16	6	1	16	0	1	10	0	1	8	0	1	10	0	1	14	6	2	0	6	2	3	0	2	15	0
0	0	7¼	0	0	8¼	0	0	8¼	0	0	7½	0	0	7¼	0	0	8	0	0	8½	0	0	10	0	0	9	0	0	7½	0	0	8½
0	1	4	0	1	4	0	1	4	0	1	3	0	1	3	0	1	4	0	1	5	0	1	6	0	1	3½	0	1	6	0	1	6
0	0	8	0	0	8½	0	0	9	0	0	8	0	0	8	0	0	8	0	0	9	0	0	9	0	0	8	0	0	8½	0	0	10
0	4	6	0	4	6	0	4	6	0	4	0	0	4	0	0	3	8	0	3	8	0	3	8	0	3	6	0	3	6	0	3	6
0	1	4	0	1	4	0	1	4	0	1	4	0	1	4	0	1	4	0	1	4	0	1	4	0	1	4	0	1	4	0	1	4
0	0	5¼	0	0	5½	0	0	5½	0	0	5¼	0	0	5	0	0	5	0	0	5	0	0	5	0	0	4½	0	0	4½	0	0	4½
0	0	7	0	0	7¼	0	0	7¼	0	0	6½	0	0	6	0	0	6¼	0	0	6	0	0	6¼	0	0	6¼	0	0	6¼	0	0	4½
0	0	4½	0	0	4½	0	0	4½	0	0	4½	0	0	4½	0	0	4½	0	0	4½	0	0	4½	0	0	4½	0	0	4½	0	0	4½
0	0	7	0	0	7½	0	0	7½	0	0	8	0	0	7½	0	0	7½	0	0	8¼	0	0	8	0	0	7½	0	0	7½	0	0	8½
0	0	7½	0	0	7½	0	0	7½	0	0	7½	0	0	7½	0	0	8	0	0	8	0	0	8½	0	0	7½	0	0	7	0	0	9
0	0	1¼	0	0	1⅜	0	0	1½	0	0	1⅜	0	0	1¼	0	0	1⅛	0	0	1¼	0	0	1⅜	0	0	2	0	0	2⅛	0	0	1⅜

CHAP. VII.

15*s.* to 40*s.* per week, pay on the average one day's wages in rent; that below 25*s.* per week, this proportion is rather more than less; and that the increase in the latter case, during the last twenty years, has ranged from twenty to thirty per cent., chiefly owing to the augmented local taxation which, in the case of the labouring classes, is now not less, on the average, than one fifth of their rent.

CHAPTER VIII.

COMPARISON OF THE COMMERCIAL PROGRESS OF NATIONS.

CHAP VIII.

Our export trade compared with that that of other countries.

THE relative progress of the export trade is the most reliable standard by which the cost of production in different countries may be compared. If we apply this test to our own case, we shall find no reason to complain of the measure of success which has attended British enterprise in competition with foreign industry.

In the long period of depression which followed upon the panic of 1866, we were told by many who doubted the recuperative powers of English industry, that we should never again recover our former prosperity; and that foreign competitors had driven us from the field never to return again. The marvellous commercial activity of the last years must have dispelled these misgivings, and should make our toiling millions and their employers grateful for the measure of success which has attended British enterprise, in competition with foreign industry. While the more recent revival of our trade must be admitted to be highly satisfactory; yet when we look back upon the commercial success of England through an extended cycle of years, the growth of our trade becomes still more remarkable. In 1800, according to a calculation by M. Chemin Dupontes, the entire exports of the Western nations, including the United States, to and from the East, amounted in value to 16,000,000*l.* sterling, while the total value of the trade between the West and East in 1860 amounted to 112,000,000*l.* sterling; and this large sum was again increased in 1866 to 161,000,000*l.* sterling, the increase being in round numbers 49,000,000*l.* The whole of the recent gain has been secured by Great Britain; and if a comparison be made between England and France for the entire period, it appears that, while in the last sixty

CHAP. VIII.

years the trade of England to the East has increased tenfold, that of France has not even doubled.

General growth of trade.

Professor Levi.

The recent valuable work of Professor Leone Levi furnishes conclusive evidences of the growth of our commercial prosperity. The superiority of England over every competitor in the industrial field is sufficiently proved by the proportion of our exports per head of the population. In England the rate is 6*l.* 3*s.* 2*d.*, while in France it is only 2*l.* 18*s.* 3*d.*, and in Italy 1*l.* 4*s.* 8*d.*

The general result of the progress of British commerce is summarised in the following recital of the principal achievements of the past century :—

In 1763 the population probably was 10,000,000. In 1870 it was 31,000,000, showing an increase of 326 per cent. But if the population has increased three times, the imports have increased thirty times, namely, from 10,000,000*l.* to 303,000,000*l.*; the exports nearly twenty times, namely, from 13,000,000*l.* to 244,000,000*l.*; the navigation of ports fifteen times, namely, from 1,500,000 tons, to 36,000,000 tons; and the shipping belonging to the kingdom fourteen times, namely, from 550,000 tons to 7,100,000 tons. The whole trade of the kingdom actually doubled itself during the last fifteen years, having grown from 260,000,000*l.* in 1855, to 547,000,000*l.* in 1870.

Investments in railways the best evidence of our prosperity.

The sum invested in railways in 1845 was 88,000,000*l.* In 1870 the capital embarked amounted to 530,000,000*l.* The increase most fully demonstrates the growth of capital, the vastness of our accumulations, and the extent of our industrial resources.

Alleged decay of ship-building in England.

During the last panic, ship-building on the Thames was almost entirely discontinued. The high wage paid to shipwrights in London was assigned as the reason for the decay of their industry, and it was affirmed that our ship-builders were no longer able to build vessels as cheaply as their competitors abroad. I have spared no pains to test the value of these assertions, that were too readily believed by the credulous public; and the following statement embraces the more important results of the enquiry.

CHAP. VIII.

Austrian Lloyd's.

The fleet of the Austrian Lloyd's Company contained 68,450 tons of shipping. Of this total 17,705 tons were built at Trieste, 3,300 at Stettin, 1,420 at New York, 33,110 at Glasgow, 7,170 in London, 2,580 at Newcastle, 1,240 at Bristol, and 1,050 at Liverpool. Thus in round figures there were 44,000 tons of British-built shipping, out of an entire fleet of 68,450 tons. In Italy there were four companies receiving subsidies from the state for carrying the mails. The total tonnage of the vessels belonging to the four companies was 35,089 tons. Two vessels of the combined tonnage of 1,150 tons were built at Marseilles, while all the other steamers were constructed in England.

Azizieh Line.

The principal line of steamers subsidised by the Egyptian Government, the Azizieh Line had (i.e. at the date of my enquiry two years ago) a fleet consisting of 31,249 tons of shipping. Of this total, one ship of 2,617 tons was built in Austria, one of 750 tons in Holland, one of 300 tons in Antwerp; while all the other ships were built in England.

In the port of Marseilles there were numerous merchant steamers not subsidised by the Government. Of the total tonnage, 20,290 tons were built in England, and only 16,467 tons in France.

CHAP. VIII.

Messageries Impériales.

The fleet of the Messageries Impériales possessed 50,547 tons of shipping. Since 1864 no steamers had been built in England. Restrictions were imposed, as the condition of granting an increased subsidy, which compelled the company to build all their ships in France; but the fleet of the Messageries Impériales still contains 10,420 tons of English built shipping.

Compagnie Transatlantique.

The Compagnie Transatlantique was not at its first foundation precluded from purchasing steamers abroad. Of their entire fleet, consisting of twenty-four ships, fifteen were built in England.

British Steam Navigation Company.

The British Indian Steam Navigation Company, although an English Company, had invited tenders from all the principal shipbuilders abroad, and they invariably went to the cheapest market. The total tonnage of their ships was 21,759 tons. All were built in England, and all, with one exception, in the

CHAP. VIII.

Netherlands India Company.

Clyde. The Netherlands India Company, a perfectly neutral company, and wholly free from British proclivities, had a fleet of 7,875 tons, but only two small vessels of that fleet were built in Holland. The remainder were from the Clyde. The line of steamers running from Hamburgh to New York included eleven vessels of a total tonnage of 22,000 tons. All but the Allemannia were built by Mr. Caird.

North German Lloyd's Company.

The fleet of the North German Lloyd's Company, composed of thirteen vessels of 26,000 tons, was constructed entirely by Mr. Caird.

At Bordeaux, of the unsubsidised foreign going steamers, four were trading to Rotterdam and two to Amsterdam, under the Dutch flag; and nine vessels were trading to Hamburgh and Havre under the French flag. All these steamers were built in England.

Rubattini & Co.

MM. Rubattini & Cie. of Genoa, were building four steamers to trade between Genoa and India. Of these three were being constructed at Newcastle, and one in Glasgow.

Another company had lately been formed to run between Italy and the River Plate. All their steamers were being built by Messrs. Dudgeon & Co. on the Thames.

These examples are merely quoted as illustrations. The general result of the progress of ship-building in England is exhibited, though in less minute detail, in the Board of Trade return. In 1861 7,487 tons of shipping were built for foreigners. In 1863 the tonnage had increased to 17,320 tons, as compared with 365,000 tons built for the home trade. In 1868 the proportion built for foreigners was much larger, having increased to 46,000 tons, as compared with 316,000 tons built for the home trade. In conclusion, it may be affirmed that the opinion expressed by the Select Committee on Merchant Shipping of 1860 is not less true at the present time than it was at the date when their report was written. It states that, in comparing the relative cost of the British shipping with that of all the various maritime countries with which we are engaged in the race of competition, there is no reason to doubt, when every point of com-

CHAP. VIII.

parison is duly taken into consideration, that the first cost of building vessels is as low in this country as in any other; while it is undoubted that steamers can be built in the United Kingdom at much less comparative expense and greatly superior to any produced abroad.

Thiers on the industrial situation in France, January 1870.

I have stated above that, in our recent commercial difficulties, the cry was too often raised that our trade, which had temporarily diminished, would never revive, and that our foreign competitors were about to establish an era of golden industry on the ruins of British industry. The speeches of M. Thiers and the Protectionists in the French Chamber as recently as 1870, describe the condition of French industry in terms which give little occasion for envious feelings in the English reader. They say that in mixed woollen and cotton stuffs England had beaten France—that we produced 10,000,000 tons of iron as contrasted with an annual production of 1,000,000 tons in France; that the French had no heavy goods to export; that having given up differential rates, they had to import all their colonial and eastern produce from England; and that the merchant navy was rapidly decaying. Comparing the relative positions of England and France, in reference to cotton manufactures, M. Thiers stated that while England worked up 3,000,000, France only worked up from 600,000 to 700,000 bales, and that the cost of production was from 15 to 20 per cent. less in England than in France. "It was," he said, "the cheap industry of Rouen which suffered most from English competition. The genius of England was for cheapness—that of France for quality."

Comparative number of spindles—M. de Forcade.

The relative importance of the cotton manufacture in the different countries of Europe was also compared by M. de Forcade in the course of the same debate. His statement gave the following results, that England had 30,000,000 spindles, France 6,800,000, the Zollverein 2,500,000, Russia 1,800,000, Austria 1,700,000, Switzerland 1,500,000, Belgium 600,000, and Italy 450,000 spindles.

The recent dullness of trade was not the

CHAP. VIII.

exceptional misfortune of this country. The same causes produced even more discouraging effects in those countries which are our most formidable competitors in commerce. It is not a little remarkable that a great part of the recent increase in our commerce has taken place in the iron trade, the branch of industry in which it had been alleged that the pressure of foreign competition had been, and would be, most particularly felt.

On a general review of the subject, the profits of trade in England in the last quarter of a century cannot but be regarded as satisfactory.

If the returns had been larger, employers would have encountered more severe competition; and though wages may be a little higher in England than abroad, our superior machinery and greater command of capital as yet compensate for the difference.

The price of locomotives not greater in England than abroad.

Particular cases have from time to time been quoted in the newspapers and elsewhere in proof of the success, with which foreigners have engaged in competition with our manufacturers in various branches of trade, and especially in the manufacture of iron and machinery, in which we were formerly unrivalled.

The experience of the Consulting Engineers of our Indian Railways does not by any means go to prove that foreign iron masters or engine builders can successfully compete with the English. Their experience, it may be added, is all the more valuable, because the Indian railways afford the most perfect example of a purely neutral market. There is no personal influence acting on the minds of Indian railway engineers and directors prejudicially to our interests; and no customs duties, which are protective to our manufacturers, are imposed upon the importation of our manufactures into India. The plant and machinery for the Indian railways are purchased in the cheapest market; and it is certain that the foreigner would be preferred regardless of national sympathies, if he could compete with the iron trade at home, either in quality or price. Let us then examine into the actual state of the facts, as regards the supply of rails and locomotives to the Indian railways.

I shall first appeal to the experience of Mr. A. M. Rendel. In November and December 1865, tenders were invited by advertisement for a large number of locomotives for the East Indian Railway. Eminent foreign as well as English makers were free to compete, and twenty-two tenders were sent in. The result was, that eighty engines, varying in cost from 3,165*l.* to 2,450*l.*, were ordered from English makers, at an average price of 2,600*l.* each; twenty from Kiessler, of Esslingen, near Stuttgart, at 2,550*l.* each; and twenty from an English maker, at 2,440*l.*; so that the foreign maker received a price intended to be intermediate between those of the English makers. It ought to be mentioned that at the date when the order was given, English houses were full of work. Not long afterwards, in consequence of the rapid development of traffic on the East Indian Railway, it became a matter of urgent importance to send out additional locomotives as early as possible. Accordingly ten more engines were ordered from an English firm at the price agreed upon in the first tender, viz., 2,450*l.*; and ten more were ordered from Esscher, Weiss, and Co., of Zurich, who undertook to make them for 2,550*l.* each, the price which had been previously accepted by the other foreign makers. At the termination, however, of their contract, Esscher, Weiss, and Co. made a representation to Mr. Rendel that they had sustained a loss, and asked to be allowed by way of compensation, to make ten more engines of the same kind, but at the enhanced price of 2,800*l.* It is therefore evident that in the results of their competition with the English makers, who were under no pressure in regard to price, all the shops being so full of work that early delivery was an impossibility, Esscher, Weiss, and Co. had little cause for satisfaction. Indeed, they admitted a substantial loss. But, even if this contract had been more satisfactory to Esscher, Weiss, and Co. than it actually proved, their success would have been largely due to British industry; seeing that

CHAP. VIII.

the boiler plates, the copper fire-boxes, the wheels, the pig-iron for the cylinders, the tubes, and the frame plates (in short, two-thirds of the materials used in the construction of their engines,) came from England in a manufactured state. It was the same with the engines supplied by Kiessler. That firm assured Mr. Rendel that they could not think of asking him to accept Prussian iron or copper, and that by far the greater portion of their material came from England. Of course, to a certain extent, this was done under the requirements of the specification; but no pressure was needed on the part of the engineers. The axles and wheel tires were specified to be of Prussian steel; but for this, they too would have been of English make. But the experience of Mr. Rendel is by no means limited to the purchase of locomotives. Rails and iron bridge work upon the largest scale have been supplied in England for the Indian railways for which he has acted; and the tenders have been obtained on all occasions, when a large order has been given, by open advertisement;

General cheapness of iron works in England as compared with the Continent.

CHAP. VIII.

and all continental makers have been as free to tender and would be accepted on the same guarantees as English makers. Yet out of the total expenditure during the last ten years, of from 7,000,000*l.* to 8,000,000*l.* sterling on materials and plant for the East Indian railways constructed under Mr. Rendel's supervision, with the exceptions I have made, the whole of these contracts have been obtained by English manufacturers.

Engines for the Punjaub Railway.

Another interesting and conclusive proof of the success with which our engine builders can compete for the supply of locomotives, is furnished by the following schedule, prepared by Mr. W. P. Andrew, of the tenders for ninety-four locomotives received by the Punjaub Railway Company, in answer to a public advertisement in January 1866:—

Tenders for Supply of Engines for the Punjaub Railway.

Country from which tender received.	Prices per engine and tender.
1 Germany	£3,156
2 England	2,990
3 England	2,960
4 England	2,950

CHAP. VIII.

Tenders for Supply of Engines for the Punjaub Railway.

Country from which tender received.	Prices per engine and tender.
5 England	2,850
6 England	2,835
7 England	2,810
8 England	2,790
9 England	2,750
10 Germany	2,750
11 England	2,685
12 Germany	2,680
13 England	2,680
14 Switzerland	2,650
15 England	2,650
16 England	2,600
17 France	2,595
18 England	2,575
19 England	2,500
20 Scotland	2,424
21 Scotland	2,395

It is not necessary to comment on this most important illustration of the relative powers of British and Continental industry. Though not yet beaten in the race, we cannot afford to disregard the pressure of competition. It is for our manufacturers to apply to the best advantage all the resources which a ready supply of the raw material and a large command of capital afford; and our operatives on their part must strenuously exert themselves to increase the productive value of their labour, else they cannot hope to retain the pre-eminence which they have hitherto enjoyed.

How engines for the Great Eastern Railway were ordered from France.

Serious alarm was felt, when, in 1865, fifteen engines were ordered for the Great Eastern Railway from MM. Schneider.

These misgivings would probably have been allayed, had it been generally known that at the same time, when the fifteen engines were ordered from Creuzot, forty other engines were ordered from English firms, and that when MM. Schneider were subsequently asked to undertake the construction of twenty-five more engines at the price they had agreed to accept for the fifteen engines originally ordered, the offer was declined.

The prices actually quoted by the various tenders are given in the following table :—

CHAP. VIII.

Tenders for fifty-five Goods and twenty-five Passenger Engines. June, 1865.

	Goods	Passenger	Mean
English Makers	£3,350	£3,350	£3,350
,, ,, ...	3,300	3,350	3,325
,, ,, ...	3,250	3,200	3,225
,, ,, ...	3,145	3,085	3,115
,, ,, ...	3,115	3,085	3,100
,, ,, ...	3,045	3,135	3,090
,, ,, ...	3,100	3,075	3,088
,, ,, ...	No tender	2,950	—
,, ,, ...	2,950	2,940	2,945
Belgian Makers	2,890	2,890	2,890
English Makers	2,889	2,790	2,840
,, ,, ...	2,745	2,695	2,720
,, ,, ...	2,730	2,590	2,660
,, ,, ...	2,600	No tender	—
Schneider, Tender for Goods and Passenger Engines together, £2,498			

The eminent English engineer at whose instance the original order was intrusted to MM. Schneider, possesses, from long residence in France, a special knowledge of French workmen; and it is his opinion that the price of that kind of labour in France was not generally cheaper for a given quantity of work than it is in England, while the material of course costs at least as much.

The following schedule of tenders for Rolling Stock for the Poti and Tiflis Railway gives no indication of the failing power

CHAP. VIII.

Tenders for the Poti and Tiflis Railway.

of British industry. The tenders were sent in three years ago, at a time when anxiety as to the future of British industry was so commonly expressed among our principal manufacturers.

CARRIAGES.

French.

First Class		Second Class		Third Class.
Fcs. 10,785	.	Fcs. 9,890	.	Fcs. 6,600

English.

£540	. .	£485	. .	£330
550	. .	490		335

All the above delivered in Poti.

ENGINES AND TENDERS.

French.

Goods		Passengers		Delivered in
Fcs. 46,320	.	42,000	.	Antwerp.

Belgian.

Fcs. 55,000	.	Fcs. 49,000	.	Antwerp.
£2,355	. .	£2,265	.	Poti

English.

£1,933	.	£1,680	..	Liverpool
2,100	.	2,000	.	Glasgow
2,125	.	1,842	.	Poti
2,195	.	2,080	.	Liverpool

CHAP. VIII.

English—continued.

Goods		Passengers		Delivered in
£2,395	.	£2,280	.	Liverpool.
2,450	.	2,300	.	"
2,575	.	2,240	.	"
2,600	.	2,400	.	"
2,950	.	2,700	.	Poti.

Comparison of the productive powers of our iron works with the home demand.

The extent to which the engine-building establishments are employed upon foreign orders may be proved by a comparison of their actual capabilities with the following estimate of the home demand for locomotives.

In the year 1865, Mr. Manby found from careful analysis of returns made to him from numerous railways, that the life of engines built by Messrs. Robert Stephenson and Co. might be taken at 480,000 miles. At that period the "Train mileage" of the United Kingdom equalled 120,000,000 miles. Then 120,000,000÷480,000=250+50 engines (for contingencies)=300 engines destroyed annually.

Since the date of Mr. Manby's calculation, railway traffic has been enormously increased.

Details of Tenders for Rolling Stock for the Poti and Tiflis Railway.

ENGLISH.

Ballast Wagons	Covered Wagons	Platform Wagons	High side Goods Wagons	Coal Wagons	Timber Wagons	Delivery
£ s. d.	£ s. d.	£ s. d.	£ s. d.	£ s. d.	£ s. d.	
64 4 6	88 16 0	64 0 0	74 12 0	66 6 0	71 3 0	Gloucester or Swansea
79 0 0	104 18 0	78 0 0	89 10 0	81 10 0	86 10 0	Gloucester
79 12 6	105 0 0	79 8 0	90 0 0	81 14 0	88 10 0	Liverpool
83 0 0	106 10 0	82 0 0	92 0 0	86 0 0	94 10 0	Ditto, or Newport
84 0 0	108 0 0	90 0 0	92 0 0	92 0 0	97 0 0	Ditto, London or Hull
90 5 0	126 0 0	94 0 0	109 10 0	97 0 0	99 10 0	Ditto, ditto
98 0 0	127 0 0	104 0 0	110 10 0	84 0 0	105 0 0	Poti
105 0 0	134 0 0	79 0 0	117 0 0	107 0 0	118 0 0	Ditto

FRENCH.

Francs	Francs	Francs	Francs	Francs	Francs	Delivery
1,850	2,350	1,825	2,100	1,917	2,159	F. O. B. Havre
2,000	2,600	1,885	2,090	1,930	2,200	Ditto, ditto
1,865	2,267	2,050	2,350	2,150	2,490	On quay ditto
2,240	2,840	2,220	2,570	2,300	2,550	F. O. B. Havre
2,130	2,950	2,240	2,650	2,340	2,600	Marseilles
2,550	3,170	2,625	2,945	2,780	3,045	Havre

BELGIAN.

Francs	Francs	Francs	Francs	Francs	Francs	Delivery
1,781	2,323	1,794	2,021	1,830	1,995	Antwerp
2,200	2,850	2,120	2,356	2,159	2,692	Ditto
2,270	2,920	2,190	2,610	2,250	2,670	Ditto

But our resources for producing locomotives, even allowing for the increase of traffic, are still very largely in excess of the demand for British railways alone. We had in 1867

CHAP. VIII.

thirty or more factories, which could supply 1,500 locomotives annually. If, therefore, these establishments are ever fully employed, as at the present time they mostly are, a large proportion of the locomotives must be exported. In 1869, immediately after the cry of alarm had been raised, large orders from abroad were received by the English manufacturers. To show how shallow were the foundations on which the apprehensions of the decay of British industry were based, I may mention that, in the case of one firm, which had up to the end of 1869 received orders for 92 engines for Russia, 70 of those locomotives were ordered in 1869, 2 in 1868, and 30 in 1864.

Alarm at the importation of rails from Belgium.

It was also said that Belgian rails were being largely imported into England. It is true that some 600 tons for the East Gloucestershire Railway were supplied by a Belgian firm in 1865. The price of these rails was 6*l.* 10*s.* per ton, delivered at Gloucester. But a solitary instance like this proves nothing as to the general comparative prices of English and Belgian rails. It was because our ironmasters were more fully employed than the ironmasters in Belgium, and because the prices of rails had in consequence fallen more rapidly in Belgium than in England, that the order in question was executed abroad.

Since the year 1865, rails have been made in England at a cheaper rate than that paid for the Belgian rails supplied to the East Gloucestershire Railway.

The fortunes of our Belgian rivals have been as chequered as those of their English ironmasters. The following table shows the fluctuations in Belgian prices :—

Average price per ton of Belgian rails.

	Francs
For 1835, average price per ton .	340,00
„ 1836 „ „ .	425,00
„ 1837 „ „ .	438,75
„ 1838 „ „ .	394,00
„ 1839 „ „ .	378,00
„ 1840 „ „ .	239,50
„ 1841 „ „ .	248,00
„ 1842 „ „ .	234,00
„ 1843 „ „ .	221,60
„ 1844 „ „ .	290,00
„ 1845 „ „ .	309,00
„ 1846 „ „ .	320,00

CHAP. VIII.

Average price per ton of Belgian rails—(continued.)

				Francs
For 1847	average price per ton		.	263,00
„ 1848	„	„	.	190,00
„ 1849	„	„	.	180,00
„ 1850	„	„	.	170,00
„ 1851	„	„	.	170,00
„ 1852	„	„	.	172,00
„ 1853	„	„	.	231,00
„ 1854	„	„	.	220,25
„ 1855	„	„	.	212,50
„ 1856	„	„	.	213,85
„ 1857	„	„	.	237,65
„ 1858	„	„	.	160,00
„ 1859	„	„	.	160,00
„ 1860	„	„	.	160,30
„ 1861	„	„	.	156,85
„ 1862	„	„	.	149,60
„ 1863	„	„	.	142,90
„ 1864	„	„	.	157,35
„ 1865	„	„	.	162,65
„ 1866	„	„	.	169,00
„ 1867	„	„	.	137,70
„ 1868	„	„	.	170,80

Iron girders.

Much has been said too from time to time as to the importation of iron girders from Belgium into this country; but Dr. Percy, in his evidence before the Committee on Scientific Education, stated that the iron girders recently imported from Belgium would be made here, if there were a larger demand. A manufacturer would not alter his mills for a special kind of girder, unless there was considerable demand; and he urged, as a sufficient reason why there should be no apprehension on this subject, the remarkable success which has been achieved in England in the production of armour plates.

It is well known that in 1869 the productive powers of our rail-rolling mills were strained to the utmost, and that almost the whole of those rails were exported.

Increased production of steel in England.

Take again the manufacture of steel. In 1851 the entire annual production of steel in Sheffield was 35,000 tons, of which about 10,000 tons were cast steel. At the present time, at the works at Barrow alone, they can turn out 1,200 tons per week of finished steel; and they will shortly incease their powers to from 2,000 to 2,400 tons of cast steel per week. England has a decided pre-eminence in this branch of metallurgy.

It has been shown that until the last year there had been no increase whatever for a

CHAP. VIII.

The increased activity of the French engineering works has caused a great rise in wages.

long period in the rate of wages in England, in the trades concerned in the building of locomotive engines; while, on the other hand, at Schneider's establishment there has been an increase during the last fifteen years of 38 per cent. We must not, therefore, look at the increase of wages for an explanation of the reason why we are no longer monopolists of the engine building trade. The real explanation is to be found in the circumstance that, as the railway system was first established in this country, so we were the first in the field as locomotive engine builders.

Our former monopoly as manufacturers of railway stock the result of our being first in the field.

When, for example, a supply of rolling stock was required for the service of the Paris and Rouen Railway, the first important railway constructed on the Continent, it was thought necessary to create the special engine building works already mentioned, at Sotteville, near Rouen, for the purpose of building the locomotives and carriages required for the line. A great number of the mechanics employed at the works were Englishmen; and the direction and supervision were exclusively English. Why was it that recourse was had to English experience in this case? Solely because the science of building locomotives was an occult science at that time on the Continent. Then, as now, labour of all descriptions was not only as cheap but much cheaper abroad than in England. It is true that the necessary experience and mechanical skill are not as yet to be found among continental mechanics. But surely it would have been unreasonable to assume that we were to remain for ever monopolists of a trade in which the foreigner only required additional experience in order to enable him to compete with our countrymen. It is because we were first in the field, and not because at a former time labour was relatively cheaper, that we, for many years after the first introduction of the railway system, supplied engines to continental countries which now supply themselves. Even now, be it remembered, our continental neighbours would draw large supplies from England, if they did not protect their own manufacturers by heavy import duties.

CHAPTER IX.

IS LABOUR BECOMING DEARER?

CHAP. IX.

Has the cost of labour increased in England during the last quarter of a century?

THE question of the rise in the wages of labour has of late come frequently under discussion. During the last thirty years the purchasing power of money, the standard of living, and the education and moral condition of the working classes have sensibly changed. It becomes therefore extremely difficult to make a satisfactory comparison of the relative cost of labour at the present time and in the early days of railways.

Wages on the earlier railway contracts.

In the year 1837 on the Penkridge viaduct on the Grand Junction Railway, the wages were for navvies from 2*s.* 6*d.* to 2*s.* 8*d.* per day, and for artisans from 22*s.* to 23*s.* per week. On the works of the Aire and

Calder Navigation, executed in 1836, navvies working in butty-gangs by piece work, earned from 4*s.* to 5*s.* and in some cases 6*s.* per day. On the London and Birmingham Railway, platelayers, working on the piece-work system, earned 5*s.* per day, and, working by the day, 3*s.* 6*d.* per day. On the Trent Valley line, completed in 1846, the wages of navvies averaged from 3*s.* to 3*s.* 6*d.*, and men employed in filling wagons were paid from 2*s.* 9*d.* to 3*s.* On the Trent Valley line on many portions of the contract, during a great part of the time during which it was being executed, the men worked night and day. At Nuneaton there was no difficulty in engaging 100 men in the course of three days to be employed in night work alone. Men could not be found to do night work so readily at the present time. A few years ago, on the Central Wales line, the wages of navvies were on the average 2*s.* 8*d.*, and of tradesmen 4*s.* per day. In 1869, in South Wales, in consequence of the long continued depression in the iron trade, wages were as low as they have ever been.

Wages in 1846.

1869.

CHAP. IX.

1871.

In the present year, on the works in progress for the widening of the London and North-Western Railway near London wages have risen considerably, in consequence of the great demand for labour in all parts of the country. The contractor for the extension, who was in my father's employ upon his first contract on the Grand Junction, gives the present rates of daily wages for navvies at from 3*s.* to 3*s.* 6*d.*, for carpenters and smiths 5*s.* to 5*s.* 3*d.*, and for masons and bricklayers 6*s.* per day. He is of opinion that, on the whole, the cost of labour is fifteen per cent. dearer than at the commencement of his career, yet by their superior skill and contrivance, the experienced contractors of the present day are able to undertake work for a smaller price than they were prepared to accept at the earlier period. Opinions, however, as to the relative cost of labour, now and in former days, are not unanimous. Those who have been engaged principally in the great towns and especially near London, have experienced much more serious difficulties, in consequence of the variations in the

Differences of opinion as to the comparative cost of labour.

price of labour, than employers who have been chiefly engaged in the rural districts. In consequence of the unprecedented demand for labour at the present time, wages are unusually high. They must of course at all times be influenced by the relation between the supply and demand. But, taking the average, it may be safely affirmed, that while the prices for railway work are nearly the same now as in the period when the London and Birmingham Railway was being made, the cost of labour is on the whole, somewhat dearer than in former days, and labour-saving appliances have not fully made up for the increase in wages.

Rise of wages in building trades in London.

The increased expenditure on building in London and other great cities, which has resulted from the augmented wealth of the country, has led to a great advance, both in London and in Manchester, in the rate of wages in the building trades.

The amount of this increase is shown in a statement prepared by Messrs. Lucas Bros. the well-known builders.

"We find," they write, "for some years

CHAP. IX.

previous to September 1853, that the rate of wages was as follows :—

	For Mechanics, Masons, Bricklayers, Carpenters and Plasterers	Labourers
Previous to 1853	5/ per day of 10 hours . .	3/ per day of 10 hours
From September 1853 to March 1861	5/6 ,, ,, . .	3/4 ,, ,,
March 1861 to September 1865	/7 per hour, or 5/10 per day	/4¼ per hour, or 3/6½ per day
September 1865 to May 1866	/7½ per hour, or 6/3 per day	/4½ per hour, or 3/9 per day
May 1866 to present time . .	/8 per hour, or 6/8 per day	/4¾ per hour, or 3/11½ per day

And we consider that the price of building is twenty-five to thirty per cent. more now than it was in 1853."

The figures given by Messrs. Lucas correspond very closely with the following statement from Mr. Broadhurst, a Trades Union officer, who, in a letter written in 1869, informed me that in 1840 the daily rate of wages in the building trades was 5*s.* per day of ten hours, or a total of 1*l.* 10*s.* for sixty hours. In 1850 the rate was 5*s.* per day of ten hours, Saturday excepted, when the men ceased work at four o'clock, being a total of 1*l.* 10*s.* for 58½ hours' work. In 1860 the rate was 5*s.* 6*d.* per day, or 1*l.* 13*s.* for 58½ hours' work. At the date of his letter it was 1*l.* 17*s.* 8*d.* per week of 56½ hours.

CHAP. IX.

Advance of wages at Manchester.

In 1837 wages advanced in Manchester from 4*s.* to 4*s.* 6*d.* per day. The working hours were, on Monday, from 7 A.M. to 6 P.M., and on the four following days from 6 A.M. to 6 P.M. On Saturday from 6 A.M. to 4 P.M. An hour and three quarters each day was allowed for meals, and the earnings were therefore 1*l.* 7*s.* for 59½ hours of work. In the spring of 1869 the wages in Manchester were 1*l.* 13*s.* for a week of 55 hours.

Explained by increased demand.

I am not in a position to pronounce judgment on the comparative cost of building. I can only give the data which have been placed in my hands. It is possible that the cost of building has increased, and that the increase is due to a rise of wages. But if an advance has taken place, it is fully explained by the extension of the metropolis, in the vast suburbs built during the last quarter of a century, and now being built. In this, as in all other cases, where a permanent rise has been established, there has been an increased competition among employers for a supply of labour, which has for a lengthened period been insufficient to meet their demand.

CHAPTER X.

INFLUENCE OF AMERICAN WAGES ON THE ENGLISH LABOUR-MARKET.

CHAP. X.

Emigration.

WHILE we have much reason to congratulate ourselves on our commercial successes in the past, it must be remembered that the competition of the American against the English employer for a supply of skilled labour from this country has already exercised and must always exert an important influence on the price of labour.

On this ground, and also because it is a most important opening for the most enterprising of our working men, no examination of the labour question would be complete in which the subject of Emigration was not considered.

In England the facilities of communication

Tendency to uniformity in the rate of wages.

which railways have afforded, have had a marked effect in equalizing the cost of labour throughout the country. The difference in the rates of pay of the operatives employed in ship-building on the Thames, the Mersey, the Tyne, and the Clyde, has diminished and will continue to diminish. The cost of living varies less than it did, and differences in the rental of land according as the available area is large or small, and in the cost of materials, will be the only elements of cost in which equality will be impossible. That which has already occurred in England will be repeated over a wider area. If wages in England, taking into account the amount of labour performed for the money paid and the cost of living, give to the English artisan a great advantage over the foreigner, foreign labour will be attracted to the English workshop.

The high wages in the United States affect the price of labour in England.

On the other hand, the cost of the voyage to the United States has been so materially reduced that the higher rates of pay which the workman receives on the other side of the Atlantic cannot but affect the price of labour here. The cost of living has increased so much since the war between the North and South that it is doubtful whether the married workman has derived any advantage from the increase in his wages. But should his position become much improved by a reduction in the cost of living without a corresponding reduction in his wages, a large number of our skilled operatives will be attracted to a field of labour where employment is to be obtained on better terms.

At the present time, although wages have reached a point almost unprecedented in our industrial history, extensive emigration is still taking place from this country to America. In this year 1872, a fine body of workmen employed on the Fermoy and Lismore Railway, 110 in number, left their work, and sailed from Cork to America. It is found at the present time extremely difficult to procure the necessary supply of labour in Ireland for the purpose of completing the railway in question.

With a more easy means of communication, a more perfect solidarity must gradually be established between the industrial classes throughout the civilised world. The international combinations of the operatives may do something to check the influx of foreign labour into England. But they can only effect that object by giving an additional impetus to the ascending movement, of late years much more rapid on the Continent than with us, in the scale of wages; and the rise of wages on the Continent will be an advantage to British industry, by making the competition with the continental manufacturer more equal than before.

Emigration to the United States.

The flow of immigration into the United States has been constantly increasing. Between July 1, 1865, and December 1868, a million emigrants entered the United States, and, during the last five years, Mr. Wells declares that there has been a greater development of the industry of that country than at any former period. As a necessary consequence there must be a more general demand for labour. Since 1865, 8,000 miles of railway have been constructed, and the present rate of increase is double what it was before 1860, being now 1,156 miles a year;

Railways.

CHAP. X.

while the growth in the goods traffic is sixteen times greater than the growth of the population. The production of pig-iron has been increased from 913,000 tons in 1860, to 1,550,000 tons in 1868. The import duties have tended greatly to raise prices; the profits of the manufacturers have been very large, and these circumstances have artificially stimulated production. The effect of these influences upon the wages of the artisans employed, is shown in the evidence of Mr. Hewitt before the Trades Unions Commissioners. He told them that the wage for puddling in Pittsburgh was from 21*s.* to 27*s.* per ton, as compared with 8*s.* 6*d.* in England, there being, notwithstanding the great increase in the cost of provisions in the United States, no corresponding difference in the cost of living. Mr. Wells gives a comparative statement of the wages in the United States as compared with the rates prevailing in England, showing that, in the iron rolling mills in 1868, wages were forty per cent. higher; in the foundries fifty-eight per cent. higher; in the shipyards forty-eight per cent.

The iron trade.

Rise of wages.

higher; in the cotton mills twenty-nine per cent. higher; and in the woollen mills twenty-five per cent. higher, than the corresponding rates in England.

Constant movement of population to the Western States.

We must further bear in mind that there is a constant emigration of operatives from the manufacturing districts of the United States to the unsettled territories of the far West.

The emigrants are men who have accumulated sufficient means to embark in agricultural enterprise, and are wearied with the toils of industrial life. To those well-to-do operatives, the boundless tracts of fertile land, still uncultivated and unoccupied, are offered for sale at a dollar and a quarter per acre. And who indeed can wonder that the seductive charms of pastoral life should be found so irresistible to the toil-worn labourer at the anvil or the loom? Nor is the effect of emigration to the United States on the rate of wages and on the supply of labour to the manufacturing industries of this country prospective merely. It is felt now, and has long been felt. Mr. Fawcett reminds us that the

CHAP. X.

Emigration from Ireland,

emigrants from Ireland to the United States remitted, between 1847 and 1864, no less than ten millions sterling. "No statistical fact," he says, "is more astonishing or more instructive." From 1841 to 1861 the population of Ireland was reduced from 8,100,000 to 5,800,000. Messrs. Herries and Creed, in their pamphlet, "Handicraftsmen and Capitalists," express an opinion exactly coinciding with that which I have formed, from information which has reached me from other sources. Admitting the impossibility of retaining skilled artisans in this country, if wages were to undergo any sensible reduction, they say that "in South Wales the value of labour is, as compared with other districts, cheaper in the extreme; which cheapness it is to be feared will not be maintained owing to the growing feeling for emigration manifesting itself among the Welsh iron-workers."

and South Wales;

not to be regretted.

Irish emigration has sometimes been regretted by those who measure our national greatness by the number of our population; but surely a destitute, and, because destitute, a disaffected population, is a discredit and a weakness, and not an honour or a strength to a nation. Is national greatness, although a truly noble object, superior in importance to the welfare of humanity? Is it not immeasurably better that a man should prosper in a foreign country than struggle miserably for existence in his native land?

Emigration from Germany to the United States.

The influence of the price of labour in the United States has been felt in this country, and no economist can doubt that it will soon be felt in those branches of industry in Germany in which the wages are so much below the English rates of pay.

Within the last fifteen years one million persons have emigrated from Hamburgh and Bremen to the United States. It is impossible to contemplate the struggles for life among the lower classes of our labouring population, and to apply ourselves to the solution of the difficult problem of pauperism, without casting a longing eye on the vast tracts of land, of great natural fertility, which are still unoccupied, and which, for the want of capital, are producing nothing for the sustenance of man.

CHAP. X.

The area of land still at the disposal of the United States, is calculated at upwards of 1,400,000,000 acres, exclusive of the Russian purchase of Alaska, which is estimated at 577,390 square miles, or 370,000,000 acres.

The price of land too high in the Australian colonies.

It is unnecessary to multiply statistics, or to enumerate the acres contained in our numerous and vast colonial dependencies. New South Wales alone contains 375,000 square miles; and a large proportion of this unoccupied territory possesses every natural advantage for agricultural development. But so long as the price of land in our Australian colonies remains at 1*l.* an acre, when 160 acres of better land can be obtained in America for nothing, it is not likely that an English tenant farmer, with only a small capital at his command, will undertake the much longer and more expensive voyage to Australia, in preference to the shorter and infinitely cheaper passage across the Atlantic to America.

Higher wages in States must attract our artisans.

To the artisan the high rates of wages in the United States present irresistible attractions. It must therefore be assumed that the stream of emigration, which has already attained such vast dimensions, would be increased in volume if a larger number of operatives had accumulated sufficient savings to enable them to pay the expense of removing themselves and their families to the opposite shores of the Atlantic.

Cost of living in the States.

With regard to the cost of living, a single man pays for his board and lodging 20*s.* a week; and one third should be deducted from the earnings, in order to make due allowance for the diminished purchasing power of money in the depreciated currency of the United States.

The working man better off in the States than in Europe.

The often expressed opinion of Mr. Wells that the present condition of the labourer in the United States is relatively speaking inferior to his condition before the war is well known to economists, but it is certain that this opinion is not universally shared by the working classes themselves. Mr. Hemans quotes the evidence of a German emigrant, who thus summed up the advantages which he had obtained by emigration to America. "I am," he said, "ever so much

CHAP. X.

better off. My earnings in Germany, as a plasterer, would be barely 3*s.* a day, while here they are from 11*s.* to 12*s.* My eldest boy, who is just sixteen, makes his 4*s.* a day already—more than I could have done myself at home—and pays me something for his board. Even my youngest of thirteen earns 8*s.* a week, while he learns a trade. In Germany neither of them would bring home a sixpence. If I were there, with my large family, I should be little better than a pauper; while here I have saved enough already to purchase a comfortable cottage, and I have something in the savings bank still."

"It is worth noting," observes Mr. Hemans, "that in this, as in every similar case which has come within my own personal knowledge, the labourer's cottage has been purchased with savings laid by since 1860." Hitherto Mr. Wells and other enlightened men have addressed the vo'ce of warning in vain to the powerful protectionist party in the Congress; but it is impossible that a people so enlightened as the Americans can long persevere in a system which, in the language of Mr. Wells, has made exchange in kind with all foreign nations almost impracticable, and rendered it necessary to pay for such foreign productions as are required, in the precious metals, or in the unduly depreciated promises of national payment.

Prospects of working men in the States. Some capital indispensable.

With so many chances of ameliorating his condition, it is not wonderful that the working man in the over-populated countries of the Old World is too often tempted to try his fortunes in the New, without having previously furnished himself with sufficient means to enable him to enter upon a new field of industry. If an emigrant lands in New York not possessing money enough to push on to the far West, where labour is scarce and therefore highly paid, he may find that his position is but little better than it was in the crowded cities of Europe. In the Eastern States he may remain weeks or even months without employment, unless he has friends on the spot to push his interests. "If," says Mr. Hemans, "an emigrant has such friends, well and good. Otherwise some capital to fall back upon, while waiting for his chance of employment, is indispensable."

In America there still is a great field for the energetic and enterprising emigrant; but he has difficulties to encounter which did not exist in the period preceding the war, when industry was not yet burdened with the dead weight of protection and heavy taxation.

In Philadelphia a respectable mechanic, his wife, and three children subsist on 2*l.* 13*s.* 3*d.* per week. A British mechanic would probably not spend more than 1*l.* 11*s.* 10*d.* A Philadelphian mechanic earns 3*l.* 6*s.* 7*d.*, and a British mechanic from 1*l.* 10*s.* to 2*l.* 2*s.* a week. This Philadelphian mechanic is therefore only slightly better off than the Englishman. It cannot, therefore, be surprising to hear that the Consulate at Philadelphia is besieged by Englishmen clamouring for assistance, or applying for the means of returning home. The same class, who would fail in London, fail from the same cause in the United States. If the reward of success is more liberal, more energy of character is required than in the more settled communities of the Old World.

The United States a great field for men of enterprise.

Mr. Connolly, formerly an operative mason, who has recently visited the United States, confirms, by the description he has lately given in a letter to the "Daily Telegraph," the views expressed by our consular representative. He says that "the working people in New York were never better off than during the period between 1842 and 1860. Wages in some trades have advanced since the war in a greater ratio than the cost of provisions; but thirty per cent. of the working people are unemployed. Engineers and mechanics are not much in demand; and he had invariably found that when a trade assumed the character of an industry, the men were not better paid than in England. There are more men," he says, "out of work here at present than in London in proportion to the population; yet if I had to begin the world again, this would be the country for me, with its boundless and undeveloped resources. But I would not stay in New York or in any of the larger cities. A man who

CHAP. X.

is not an agriculturist should make his home in some small but rising town, where, if there was anything in him, he would be sure to rise with its growth."

The Australian Colonies as a field for Emigration.

From the United States, let us turn to our own colonies in Australasia. In New South Wales the rates of wages are high; but a large proportion of the workpeople are unable to find regular employment. The Earl of Belmore says, in a recent Report, that there is no opening in that colony at the present time except to men of good character, and who are accustomed to hard work. As a remedy for the great distress which lately prevailed at the East End of London, emigration would have been found, by reason of the latter condition mentioned by Lord Belmore, to be an ineffectual resource.

In the opinion of Mr. Watson, an agent employed on the East London Railway, the artisans and labourers in the Iron Works at the East End of London were lamentably ill fitted for other work; and not 50 per cent. of their number would be capable of bringing allotments of land into proper cultivation.

It must further be remembered that very few paupers are able-bodied workmen. Of 163,700 persons, recently in receipt of relief from the Poor Law Board, not more than 35,000, or 38 per cent., were out-door paupers.

In South Australia we are told by Sir James Ferguson, that there is no opening in the northern territory for the ordinary labourer from Europe; although the colony presents a promising field for the investment of capital. The report of the Hon. W. Fox from New Zealand is equally discouraging to those philanthropic persons who look to emigration as an outlet for the surplus population of the United Kingdom. Even in Canada, where it is said that from 30,000 to 40,000 emigrants might be annually absorbed, there is the same demand for men with capital, and the same apprehension of the introduction of an inferior class of workmen, who, if they had failed to earn their livelihood in the United Kingdom, would be equally certain to fail in a wilder country, in which energy and industry are still more essential.

CHAP. X.

Reasons why emigrants from Great Britain are attracted to the United States.

The average annual emigration from Great Britain in the ten years preceding 1857, was 275,000. In the next decennial period the number fell to 162,000. Three-fourths of these British emigrants have gone to the United States. The emigrants who have already left our shores are the pioneers of the emigration of the future. They invite and assist their friends whom they have left, to follow them to the land of their adoption. The working man is well aware of the difficulties which beset the solitary exile in his first hard struggle in an unknown land. He naturally prefers to go to a country in which he may count upon receiving friendly counsel and advice. It is therefore probable that North America will, for many years to come absorb by far the greater number of that superior class of emigrants who possess both capital, skill, and enterprise ; are able therefore to earn a competency at home; and yet are prepared, for the sake of improving their condition, to submit to the sacrifices which expatriation involves.

The small success which has attended the

CHAP. X.

Central Argentine Land Company.

efforts recently made by the Central Argentine Land Company to induce persons to emigrate from this country to the River Plate, may be accepted as evidence that English emigrants are but little disposed to risk their fortunes in an unknown land. The advantages offered to emigrants by the company are considerable; and the average wages in the country, taken together with the moderate cost of living, are much higher than the rates paid in England. Bricklayers earn 6*s.* a day; joiners and blacksmiths, 6*s.* 6*d.*; labourers, 4*s.* 6*d.*; and railway labourers, 6*s.* The soil is fertile, the climate is healthy and agreeable, and the lands offered in allotments to emigrants possess the advantage of railway communication with a convenient port. The company is prepared to pay a portion of the emigrant's passage money, to cover the freight on his agricultural implements, and to furnish him with subsistence until the first harvest after his arrival. The rent of land is 1*s.* and the selling price 1*l.* an acre. It will be seen from the following return, that while these temptations have utterly failed to induce emi-

CHAP. X.

gration from England, a large number of persons have recently emigrated to the River Plate from Italy and France.

Emigration to the River Plate.

	1868.	1869.
From Genoa	10,000	15,000
" France . . .	8,700	16,500
" Spain . . .	3,300	5,000
" England . . .	1,096	708
Totals .	23,096	37,208

The Argentine Provinces have apparently become a favourite settlement for Italian emigrants. But, Englishmen as yet are unwilling to go, and that mainly because so few of their countrymen have settled in those countries.

It has been stated elsewhere that 2,000 men were selected in England and Scotland and taken out to Queensland, at a cost of 17*l.* per man, to be employed in the execution of a railway in that country.

Mr. Wilcox's evidence.

Mr. Wilcox, the agent under whose supervision the work was completed, says that most of the men selected remained until the completion of the works, and on the whole conducted themselves very fairly.

The artisans were still in the colony, but the majority of the labourers will only remain there as long as there is anything being done in the way of public works. Railway labourers, as far as his experience goes, do not make good colonists. The roving habits they acquire quite unfit them for becoming settlers.

General view of the prospects of emigrants.

After carefully considering the reports of the most competent observers on the condition of the labour market in the United States and in our own Colonies, and taking into view the extreme fluctuations in the demand for labour, and the discouraging position of many independent branches of industry in the eastern states of America, even a zealous philanthropist must hesitate to give his sanction to any proposals for State-aided emigration on a large scale. It is obvious that a workman may find himself worse off than at home if he lands in any one of our Colonial settlements, or in the United States, without sufficient capital to

State-aided emigration.

CHAP. X.

support him during the interval of time which may probably elapse before he obtains employment. Some capital is equally necessary, to furnish the means of travelling into those remoter districts in which alone skilled labour is paid at the higher rates.

It would be inexpedient, therefore, for the Colonial Governments, still less would it be humane or statesmanlike for the Home Government to encourage emigration, unless it were certain that employment could be offered to the emigrants, on their first arrival in a colony.

Distressed English navvies in Rouen.

One of the earliest recollections of my boyhood is the painful spectacle I beheld, when I stood by my father's side, in the Boulevard of Rouen surrounded by hundreds of famishing English workmen. There had been an unavoidable interval between the completion of his first contract in France and the commencement of the works for the extension of the railway from Paris to Rouen and on to Havre. It happened too that at that time there was but little employment for workmen in the construction of railways in England.

The navvies, who are not a provident class, had not saved money enough to support themselves for many weeks without work; and their sufferings, which would have been great in England, were aggravated in a foreign country. Soup kitchens were opened, and every effort was made to alleviate their distress; but philanthropy is no adequate substitute for brisk and well-paid employment; and the memory of that dreadful winter makes me shudder at the prospect of the sufferings which might be endured, if by Government assistance a large number of emigrants were induced to go abroad, only to find on their arrival in a remote and unknown country that it was impossible to obtain employment.

Only the thrifty and industrious succeed as emigrants.

State-aided emigration of doubtful advantage.

An examination of the Reports recently laid before Parliament will confirm the opinion generally entertained by all who have any practical knowledge of the openings for English labour in our Colonies and in foreign countries. The expenditure of public money in assisting emigration can only be justified when the persons assisted are in an indigent and helpless condition. But this is the very class which the Colonial Governments absolutely decline to receive. The emigrants who succeed, belong to the class which rarely fails to find employment at home, and is happily seldom seen by the guardians of the poor. As a general rule, we must dismiss from our minds the idea of finding in emigration a remedy for pauperism. If the State offers inducements to the working people to try their fortunes in foreign lands, it cannot divest itself altogether of responsibility for their success in the new sphere which they have been encouraged to enter.

On several occasions, as the history of my father's enterprises has shown, the sending out of a large number of workmen from England has been a successful operation. But those have been cases in which there has been a large contract in progress, and when the services of the workmen were immediately required. It is probable that the Colonies would derive advantage from the execution of numerous public works not as yet undertaken. It is possible also that arrangements might be made on terms mutually beneficial to the Colonies and to the mother country, for lending money to the Colonial Government for the purpose of carrying out such works. The expediency of such a policy may be especially deserving of consideration at a time when the field of employment in this country is contracted by the pressure of commercial distress. To this limited extent, State-aided emigration may be desirable; but an attempt to send workmen to the Colonies in sufficient numbers to give any sensible relief to the labour-market of this country in a time of wide-spread distress, would be strongly opposed by the Colonies, calamitous to the emigrants, and in the end ineffectual as a remedy for pauperism.

It is a painful task to oppose any well-intentioned proposals for ameliorating the condition of the poor; but we must be cautious, lest, in the desire to be generous, we are tempted to encourage impracticable schemes, and to excite in the minds of the people expectations which can only be realised by their own strenuous and independent exertions.

Poverty and misery there will always be, and it is our Christian duty to relieve the suffering and distressed; but, in so far as those sufferings originate in a want of employment for those who are able and willing to work, the evil is one which continually tends to remedy itself. The interference of the State by diminishing the incentives to prudence would tend rather to extend the evils it was designed to remedy, and in the end be productive of more harm than good.

Emigration has been, and will continue to be, an invaluable outlet for our redundant population; but the choice of a field of labour, and the season for emigration, must be left to the keen intelligence of the people. Pecuniary aid should not be denied in appropriate cases; but the emigrant who cannot provide the means of paying the very moderate sum now required for a passage across the Atlantic, will rarely possess that little store of capital which is an almost essential condition to successful emigration.

CHAPTER XI.

ALLEGED PHYSICAL DETERIORATION OF THE LABOURER.

CHAP. XI.

Alleged physical deterioration of the labourer.

THERE is as much difficulty in pronouncing a definite opinion upon the alleged deterioration of the labourer physically, as in estimating the difference in the cost of manual labour. Here again, employers who have of late been chiefly concerned in carrying out works near London, entertain a less favourable opinion of the labourers of the present day than other equally experienced contractors who have been engaged in the neighbourhood of provincial towns and in the rural districts. The facts which I have been able to ascertain in relation to this branch of my general subject, have chiefly reference to one kind of labourer,

CHAP. XI.

the Navvy. I am, however, strongly of opinion that most of the inferences derivable from these facts will, with certain modifications, apply equally to all classes of labourers. Mr. Milroy, whose recent experience has been chiefly in Scotland, says that, "Comparing the navvies of to-day with those we had on the Great Northern Railway, they are just as powerful physically, but they are more difficult to manage." Mr. Ballard, whose experience has been chiefly in the Midland Counties, says: "The navvies of the present day exhibit no signs of deterioration, and more work has been done in the latter days of railway construction than was formerly accomplished for the same money. The prices on the Great Northern for earthwork averaged from 1*s.* to 1*s.* 3*d.* per yard. On the Bedford line, executed some ten years ago, for much more expensive work, the prices in no case exceeded 11*d.* per yard. On the Great Northern Railway 1*s.* 6*d.* would have been charged for the same work.

Another large contractor, long associated with my father, whose experience has of late been chiefly in London, says, "that at Macclesfield, in 1847, for excavating an unusually heavy cutting, a large body of men from Lincolnshire were employed. Not one of those men was under 5 feet 10½ inches in height; such a body of men could not be found in the present day on public works." The fair inference from the testimony of these very competent authorities on this subject would appear to be that there cannot have been any marked and general diminution of physical power in the present generation of manual labourers; though the enervating life which the working population of great cities are apt to lead has diminished the physical powers of the navvies who have been employed in the metropolitan districts.

High pay of navvy leads in many instances to intemperance.

It has been alleged that the navvy is only enabled to earn his higher wages by excessive exertion. It is true that the amount of labour performed by the navvy in a day involves considerable exertion; but the men, being of powerful frame, and having great muscular development, are enabled to accomplish their work, without undue exertion, and

CHAP. XI.

are often able to go home, their day's work accomplished, at three o'clock in the afternoon. If there be special danger to health in the occupation of the navvy; it is because his large earnings admit of greater indulgence in the public-house.

At the present time, in consequence of the unusual demand for labour, employers are obliged to humour their men in every way. On a railway now being executed near Wolverhampton the men require a payment of half-a-crown on account, technically called a 'sub,' every night. The result of this practice is, that the men spend every evening in the beer-shop.

Three years ago wages were much lower than they are now, and the men were more temperate in their habits. A large proportion of the improved wages of the working class is unhappily being expended in the public-house.

There is an evil in the frequent payment of wages, in consequence of the unfortunate disposition of the navvy to resort at once to places of enjoyment, as soon as he has received his pay—If you pay wages weekly on Saturday, it rarely happens that any considerable amount of work is performed on the Monday. On the Trent Valley Railway, payment of wages took place, at the commencement of the line, once a month. The pay-day was followed by the same incapacity for exertion which is unhappily still observable. The workmen then as now, could never fill the same number of wagons for two or three days after the pay. On the Rouen and Havre Railway the pay took place once a month on a Saturday. For two or three days after the pay, the English navvy could never be induced to work. On the Barentin Viaduct, which was distant about twelve miles from Rouen, a large number of Englishmen were employed. Special omnibuses were run between Barentin and Rouen on the Sunday following the pay Saturday. On one of these omnibuses, called by the navvies the Great Western, 60 navvies could ride. These English workmen used to crowd into the streets of Rouen where they were tempted

Trent Valley.

Havre and Rouen Railway.

CHAP. XI.

to spend their hard earned wages in the numerous cafés and cabarets. The result of these excesses was, that after the pay, the horses were never taken out of the stable to draw the wagons from the cuttings until Wednesday morning.

Effect of residence in London.

It has been observed that navvies employed in the vicinity of London often lose some of their former physical strength. The temptations of a great city, which are so hard to resist, have told upon the physical condition of the railway labourer. When the works connected with the great drainage scheme of the metropolis were in progress, a large number of men were employed in the principal streets of London, and they were unable to resist the temptations of the public-houses on either side of the street, in which they were working. It must not be supposed that this gloomy picture faithfully represents the habits of all railway labourers, but it is unhappily a fair representation of the habits and condition of many of their number.

The agricultural labourer in numerous

instances is not more able to resist temptation than the navvy employed on the railways. In counties where the farm labourer is paid a portion of his wages in cider, as is the case in Devonshire and Herefordshire, drinking takes place to a terrible extent.

Work of navvy and farm labourer compared.

The nature of the occupation of the navvy is not necessarily detrimental to health. He is rarely called upon to work in the rain. In point of fact, the excavation of a cutting, or the formation of an embankment, could not be carried on with advantage either to the contractor or to his workmen, in wet weather. It may sometimes happen that a navvy is required to work in a cutting, in which his feet sink deeply into wet clay; but the agricultural labourer throughout his day's work frequently fares no better, and he rarely goes home in the intervals of his work; whereas, the navvy is in the habit of going home and changing his wet clothes.

It must be admitted that the degree of exertion to which the navvy is accustomed, is too severe for the agricultural labourer, until he has become accustomed to the more

CHAP. XI.

arduous occupation. When an agricultural labourer begins to work on a railway, he will lie down at 3 o'clock in the afternoon, fatigued and incapable of continuing his work; but, after an interval of 12 months, with more constant muscular exertion, receiving higher wages, and having better food, he will get into better condition, and will be able to perform his task without difficulty.

Good pay and food required to produce physical strength.

It has been repeatedly proved in Belgium, France, and England, that, after a sufficient interval of time, the agricultural labourer becomes perfectly master of the work required on a railway. To expect an ill-paid and lightly worked agricultural labourer to be at once capable of sustaining the exertion which a navvy is fully able to bear, would be as unreasonable as it would be to take a horse direct out of a clover field, and drive him for a long journey at a great rate of speed. It is supposed that, because there are not a great number of old navvies about, their occupation is necessarily prejudicial to health. It must be remembered that thousands of the navvies who were employed on the earlier railways, have emigrated to Australia and America. Numbers of men went to the Colonies, on the completion of the Great Northern Railway, and other railways, which were finished about the same time. As many as 350 navvies have been known to sail in one ship from Liverpool to Australia at that period.

Navvies have emigrated,

Fortunately too, many navvies have risen to a better position in life. Many of those employed by my father as navvies became afterwards platelayers, then inspectors, and afterwards sub-contractors, or small contractors on their own account. Those who have been long connected with railway construction, tell me that they know many navvies, who have attained to a great age.

and risen in life.

In the old days, when the butty-gang system was in vogue, there were numerous cases in which the men were overworked, but the cause of their being overtasked was not the pressure brought upon them by their employers. The members of the butty-gang, who divided their earnings equally among themselves, were naturally averse to allowing

Butty-gangs.

CHAP. XI.

an inferior man to enter the gang. The gangs were paid at various rates according to the amount of work performed. Those, who could get through the greatest amount of work in a day earned the highest rates of wages; and it was naturally therefore an object of ambition with a navvy to become a member of the best paid gang. But these well paid gangs were equally determined not to admit any man into their gang unless he could perform as much work as those who were already members. Men often over exerted themselves in order to be admitted into a gang composed of men of greater physical strength than themselves.

CHAPTER XII.

FLUCTUATIONS OF WAGES.

CHAP. XII.

Fluctuations in the demand for labour in England.

IT is with the deepest regret that views have been propounded in a former chapter of this work in opposition to the arguments of philanthropists who have advocated State-aided emigration, because it must be acknowledged by all who have studied these questions, that our working class is exposed to an amount of suffering from the fluctuations in the commerce of this country to a degree unparalleled elsewhere. An increase or a reduction of the pay of the working men will follow, it is true, the varying course of trade in natural sequence; but still with very inconvenient results to the internal economy of their homes. In proof of

Workmen prefer steady employment.

the preference shown by the working classes for a more moderate rate of wage with constant employment, it is interesting to compare the rate of wages in the Dockyards with the wages paid in the private ship-building yards on the banks of the Thames. The following table, compiled by Admiral King Hall, C.B., gives the rate of wages in Sheerness Yard in the years 1849, 1859, and 1869. The table showing the current rates of wages at the corresponding period in the private yards on the Thames, was prepared by Mr. John Hughes, sometime manager of the Millwall Works.

Sheerness. Rates of Wages.

		1849	1859	1869
s. *d.*		*s.* *d.*	*s.* *d.*	*s.* *d.*
	Shipwrights	4 0	4 6	4 6
	Caulkers	4 0	4 6	4 6
	Joiners	3 6	3 10	3 10
8 0	Forgemen	7 0	Same	Same
5 9	Furnacemen	5 0		
4 8	Assistant Furnacemen	4 0		
5 2	Steam Hammermen	4 6		
6 4	Anchor Firemen, 1st class	5 6		
5 6	,, ,, 2nd class	4 9		
5 6	Double Firemen	4 9		
4 10	Single Firemen, Vicemen, and Fitters	4 3		
4 4	Hammermen, 1st class	3 9		
3 9	,, 2nd class	3 3		

The figures in the left hand margin show the pay of smiths employed ten hours a day.

Average Rates of Wages Paid at Millwall Iron Works.

	Rates of Wages during years 1851 to 1869			
	1851	1861 to 1865	1865 to 1869	1869
	per week s. s.	per week s. s.	per week s. s.	per week s. s.
Fitters	33 to 38	33 to 38	35 to 40	33 to 38
Planers	30 ,, 33	30 ,, 33	32 ,, 34	30 ,, 33
Drillers	22 ,, 27	22 ,, 27	23 ,, 28	22 ,, 27
Smiths	30 ,, 42	30 ,, 42	30 ,, 42	30 ,, 42
,, helpers	22 ,, 24	22 ,, 24	22 ,, 24	22 ,, 24
Moulders	36 ,, 38	36 ,, 38	36 ,, 40	36 ,, 40
Pattern Makers	36 ,, 39	36 ,, 39	39 ,, 42	36 ,, 39
Joiners	36 ,, 39	36 ,, 39	36 ,, 42	36 ,, 42
Shipwrights	42 ,, 48	42 ,, 48	39 ,, 42	36 ,, 39
Platers	36 ,, 42	36 ,, 42	36 ,, 42	36 ,, 42
,, helpers	21 ,, 24	21 ,, 24	21 ,, 24	21 ,, 24
Rivetters	30 ,, 32	30 ,, 32	30 ,, 32	30 ,, 32
,, helpers	20 ,, 24	20 ,, 24	20 ,, 24	20 ,, 24
Caulkers	30 ,, 33	30 ,, 33	30 ,, 33	30 ,, 33
Chippers	28 ,, 30	28 ,, 30	28 ,, 30	28 ,, 30
Angle Iron Smiths	38 ,, 40	38 ,, 40	38 ,, 40	38 ,, 40
Boiler Makers	36 ,, 42	36 ,, 42	36 ,, 42	36 ,, 42
,, helpers	21 ,, 24	21 ,, 24	21 ,, 24	21 ,, 24
Painters	21 ,, 30	21 ,, 30	21 ,, 30	21 ,, 30

Hours of work, 58½ hours per week.

CHAP. XII.

It may be mentioned that the average rent of men's houses in 1851 was about 16*l.* per year; and in 1865 about 20*l.* per year. These are six-roomed houses, and in most cases more than one family occupied them.

It thus appears that at a time when shipwrights in London were earning from 6*s.* 6*d.* to 7*s.* a day, the shipwrights in Sheerness Yard, men at least as skilled as those em-

CHAP. XII.

ployed by the private ship-builders, were contented with 4*s.* 6*d.* ; though they could at any time have put their tools into their baskets, and at the end of an hour and a half's journey by rail have obtained employment from the private ship-builders at the higher rate of wages.

They preferred, and with good reason, more moderate wages with a certainty of employment, to higher wages without the certainty of permanent occupation.

The recent hasty dismissals of workmen from the Dockyards are especially to be regretted on this ground, that the workmen can no longer look with the same confidence as before to their permanent connection with a government establishment; nor will they be so ready to accept lower wages in a Dockyard in consideration of the advantages of constant employment.

Wages at Sotteville and Creuzot.

The same preference for regular employment at moderate wages to a less certain employment with higher wages, manifests itself abroad, as in England. The *employés* of a Railway Company may look upon their employment, at least during good behaviour, as being almost as certain as that under a government. Thus it has happened that in the railway works at Sotteville near Rouen, there has been no advance of importance in wages for the last twenty-five years in the class of labour employed by the builders of locomotives; although there has been a great increase in the wages paid by MM. Schneider and other private employers. The rates of wages at Sotteville are quoted in the subjoined table.

It may be interesting to compare them with the wages earned by the same trades in England.

Sotteville Works.

	s.	*d.*	
Erecters, Fitters, and Turners	24	0	per week
Smiths	27	0	„
Strikers	18	0	„
Joiners	22	0	„
Modellers	23	0	„
Moulders in the Foundry .	22	6	„

The wages at a similar establishment on the largest scale in England are shown in the following table:—

CHAP. XII.

Average Rates of Wages Paid to Skilled Workmen, Locomotive Works, England.

	1859		1869	
	s.	d.	s.	d.
Fitters	28	3·15	28	7·69
Turners	28	4·57	29	3·76
Braziers	28	6·85	28	7·06
Grinders	27	6	28	10·50
Smiths	28	5	26	10·35
Boiler Smiths	31	8	30	4·50
Bricklayers	24	5·10	30	57
Saddlers	19	8	20	3
Forgemen	34	3	34	4·05
Painters	22	10	23	1·60
Moulders	29	4·50	28	5·58
Joiners, Pattern Makers, and Sawyers	24	6·18	24	4·95
Brickmakers	27	8·44	27	5·28
Total average	27	11·23	28	1·28

Every branch of industry was in an inflated condition in the period immediately preceding the last commercial crisis. The mania of speculation was equally felt, and the reaction was equally strong in all departments of business. The following table shows the amount of capital in shares and in loans which it was proposed to raise by railway and other bills, brought before Parliament in the two years preceding the last commercial crisis, and in the two years following the collapse:—

Parliamentary loans.

In 1865	£126,441,708
„ 1866	175,490,646
„ 1867	42,638,775
„ 1868	25,207,356
„ 1869	29,221,706

It is impossible that such fluctuations can occur in the rate of construction of railways and other public works, without entailing much cruel and unnecessary suffering on the labouring poor. A melancholy illustration, to which in connection with another branch of the subject, reference has already been made, of the disturbance in the labour-market caused by the inflation and subsequent collapse of trade, has been lately exhibited on the banks of the Thames.

Fluctuating demand for labour in shipbuilding yards on Thames.

The number of men employed at the principal shipbuilding yards on the Thames was, in 1860, 11,830; in 1869, 20,880; and in 1870, 3,190. Making every allowance for the faults committed by the men, the principal share of blame for the disasters of the panic must, in justice, be laid on some of their employers.

The distress of the industrial population in the Isle of Dogs from this extension of the

CHAP. XII.

ship-building business to a height which it was impossible long to sustain, cannot be exaggerated. I was asked by Mr. Pease, M.P., to send him some additional labourers to be employed in his Collieries and Iron Works in Durham. The number of applications that were received, as soon as it became known that such employment was to be obtained, afforded a melancholy proof of the extreme destitution of the people.

Applications were received every Monday and Wednesday, and on each of those days not fewer than 700 men would present themselves. Many men, who had been employed in the iron works, earning 7*s*. a day, were anxious to go down to Durham to work as common labourers. Fine, ablebodied young men would come to the office, who had not had a day's work for upwards of two months.

General inflation of trade, before the late panic.

Over production has not been confined to ship-building on the Thames. Previous to the last commercial crisis, production had been unduly stimulated in every branch of British industry. And then, when the reaction took place, and prices had fallen from the markets having been overstocked, we were told that the price of labour and foreign competition were the causes of our inevitable misfortunes. But, as it was well said by an able and candid writer in the "Leeds Mercury," "If foreign competition were the cause of our distress, we should be justified in expecting that, in countries competing successfully with us, the manufacturers would be in a prosperous state." This was not the case. All were calling out at the same time that they were ruined by foreign competition.

A similar opinion was expressed by the Halifax Chamber of Commerce, who said that it was demonstrable that the great cause of the depression and the unremunerative character of the worsted trade had been the too rapid increase of machinery, both in spinning and weaving, which were stimulated both by permanent and temporary causes; such as the French Treaty and the American war.

British spirit of enterprise a cause of fluctuating

The same remarks would equally apply to the iron trade, and all the other leading industries of the country. The very spirit of enter-

CHAP. XII.

demand for labour.

prise, which has made England what she is, tends to produce great fluctuations in the labour market. When trade is good, our iron founders and cotton spinners are only too ready to increase the productive resources of their establishments. This leads to over-production, and ultimately to a cessation of demand from abroad. It cannot be doubted that this spasmodic and fluctuating character of our trade produces an unhappy effect upon the operatives who are subject to its influence, of a constant fluctuation in their wages.

Extinction of hand-loom weavers.

The operative class have of late suffered from another cause. Small producers, who were earning a livelihood by manual labour, have gradually been overwhelmed by the superior powers of machinery. Free trade and open competition, by reducing prices, have been good for the public at large; but, as usual the few have suffered for the benefit of the many. I will take, as an example, the distressed condition of the small weavers at Coventry, as described by Mr. Alexander Carter. The French Treaty precipitated

CHAP. XII.

Coventry.

an event which had been impending for some time, viz., the extinction of the class of small individual weavers, who worked looms that they possessed, on their own account. These men, who were, of course, but small capitalists, were either unable or unwilling, or probably both, to adapt themselves to the altered circumstances which the rest of the world saw were gradually working to the detriment of the then existing state of things, both as regards modes of labour and change of fashion. Their better educated and more active competitors on the Continent were gradually cutting them out. Formerly, the majority of ribbons were broad, and were made in a small description of loom. Narrow ribbons next came into fashion. The old looms could not be adapted to produce the narrow ribbons, and many of the weavers were unable to afford to buy new looms. The French Treaty, by taking away the last remnant of protection, of course precipitated their destruction. The only people able to contend against its effects were the large manufacturers, who were possessed of capital; were accustomed to acquaint themselves with the change of fashion by a wide range of observation; could foresee what was wanted; and could provide for the new demands of the public. It is to be feared that the industrial history of Coventry, for some years before and after the negotiation of the French Treaty of Commerce, was the old story of British obstinacy and resistance, which, though good on the field of battle, is not equally valuable in trade. It is a new story also, one not altogether satisfactory, of the extinction of the small producers, in the overwhelming competition with the large manufacturer, whose command of capital enables him to employ the most improved machinery, to procure the best designs, and to accept a lower rate of profit on a much larger production.

CHAPTER XIII.

CO-OPERATION.

Importance of a knowledge of trade and profits to workmen.

A KNOWLEDGE of markets and of the state of trade is of immense importance to the industrial classes, and it is most desirable that the course of business should be carefully watched by competent persons on their behalf. An inspection of the employers' books would be an effectual means of obtaining this knowledge. Such an inspection is permitted in Messrs. Briggs' Co-operative Colliery. Theirs is a noble experiment—but it is clear that the arrangement, experimentally adopted by Messrs. Briggs, could not, in practice, be extensively applied. In many branches of trade the returns are in the highest degree fluctuating.

Difficulties of co-operation.

CHAP. XIII.

Uncertain profits and earnings.

A cycle of years of extreme depression is followed by a period of corresponding prosperity. During the years of bad trade workmen are employed at rates of wages which involve considerable loss to the employer, who looks for his compensation to the good years of large profits. If the workmen were continually informed of the profits of their employers, I think they would be apt to exact their full share of reward in the good years, but not equally ready to submit to corresponding sacrifices in the succession of years of bad trade.

Association des Maçons.

The history of the Association des Maçons, established in Paris in 1848, is an illustration both of success in the conduct of the co-operative business, and of the difficulties inseparable from the system. Eighty-four members had been admitted, two being managers and a third assistant manager. Of the eighty-one members two thirds labour with the hod and trowel. The remainder are superintendents and distributors of work, or small holders of capital. But the society, which has been very successful in business, has found it necessary to employ from 200 to 300 men, as auxiliaries, who are paid the usual wages in the trade, but have no share in the profits. Experience unfortunately proved that when they were paid by a share in the profits, a large number of the men could not be reconciled to the losses. As a means of meeting the difficulty, which the Société des Maçons found to be so serious, it has been proposed that the minimum rate of weekly wages should be fixed in the co-operative society, and that a dividend on the profits should be declared quarterly. It has been objected to this plan that, as the workman's share of the profits is determined by the cost of manual labour, and this must be fixed by the assent of all the members of the co-operative society, a direct conflict of interest inevitably arises between them and the capitalists, in fixing the standard of the provisional remuneration which they are to receive.

Encouraging examples of co-operation.

But notwithstanding all the difficulties which beset the introduction of co-operation, the recent Blue Book, on the industrial classes abroad, is full of encouraging examples of co-

CHAP. XIII.

operative organization. It has been largely and successfully developed both in Vienna and in North Germany, under the energetic guidance of M. Schultse de Litsch. If only the difficulties above mentioned could be overcome, there cannot be a doubt that in the adoption of the co-operative principle, modified to suit the different circumstances of different trades, we shall find the only means of effecting a fusion between the otherwise contending interests of labour and capital. It has been said that an inspection of the employers' books would be an effectual means of imparting to the operatives a correct knowledge of the condition of trade, and would, in many cases, afford the means of proving the utter impossibility of allowing an advance of wages, which the workmen had claimed from ignorance of the actual state of business. But an inspection of the employers' books involves many difficulties. Take the case of the peculiarly hazardous business of a railway contractor. In some of his contracts the profits will be large, in others he will be a serious loser. A large employer taking a

Inspection of books.

general view of his affairs, and setting the good contracts against the bad, is content if the general result is satisfactory. Is it likely that the navvy, who works equally hard both on the bad contract and on the good, would be disposed to suffer a reduction of pay on the bad contract, and to see his fellow-workman employed elsewhere, but working no harder, receive double the pay awarded to himself? On the other hand, this is certain, that while the navvy upon the unsuccessful contract would object to such a reduction of pay as would protect the employer from loss, the navvy on the good contract, if he were made aware of the profits, would demand some share in those profits, in the form of an increase in his pay. Such being the practical difficulties in the way of opening the ledger of the capitalist to the inspection of the operative, what other means are available to enable the workmen to determine the fair rate of wages? The political economy of the wages question is simple enough. The difficulties which beset the question lie entirely in the practical application of the prin-

CHAP. XIII.

ciples to the facts. The facts are unhappily unknown to the working men. They have to struggle in the dark, and have no means of estimating correctly the profits of their employers.

Co-operation the only substitute for such inspection.

How, then, is this knowledge of the state of trade to be obtained by the working classes, from a source on which they might rely? Only by the introduction into every trade of the co-operative principle. The co-operative principle has hitherto been applied principally to retail trade. But it is to the more difficult organization of productive industry, that we must look for the settlement of disputes as to wages. I do not expect a general substitution of co-operative industry for private enterprise. It is impossible to deny the superior efficacy of individual to co-operative enterprise. Moreover, a considerable capital is necessary, in order that every mechanical improvement may be adopted. Again, the skill required to manage a large establishment cannot be obtained without paying high salaries; and workmen may sometimes find it difficult to obtain the necessary commercial faculty and experience either in a committee of management, or in an individual manager of their own class. Some may object to give to a fellow-workman for his services as manager a salary proportionate to his responsibility. Admitting these difficulties to be considerable, they can scarcely be regarded as insurmountable.

Letter of M. Schultse de Litsch.

M. Schultse de Litsch, the father of co-operation in Germany, has described the origin and history of the movement in a letter to the recent Co-operative Congress. While his narrative reveals the extreme difficulty of putting his admirable theory into practice, and proves that the day is yet far distant when the co-operative system can take a prominent place in the productive industry of the world, it is to be hoped that the experiments which have already been begun may not be abandoned until a more conclusive result has been obtained. The societies for supplying raw materials to artisans have not been successful. The chief cause of failure has been the neglect to insist on cash payments. On the other hand,

CHAP. XIII.

the credit societies, established to give advances of capital to persons without available property, have enjoyed a brighter fortune. These banks are now 740 in number, with a paid-up capital of 2,000,000*l.* sterling, with a sum of 8,250,000*l.* available for making loans; and they lend 29,000,000*l.* per annum.

Mr. Petre. Co-operation not practically important in Germany.

Mr. Petre, an impartial and competent observer, in a recent report to the Foreign Office, has expressed his doubt as to whether the economical results of the adoption of M. Schultse de Litsch's principle have been as important to Germany as may at first appear. But it is certain that the disputes between the partisans of M. Schultse de Litsch's principle of self-help, and those who advocate M. Lassalle's principle of State aid, have borne precious fruit in the practical education they have given to German working men in economical science.

Societies of production in France.

The societies for production in France have not been generally fortunate. Since 1848, aided by a subvention from the Government, 56 co-operative societies have been established, but only 20 were in existence in 1861.

Famili-stère de Guise.

On the other hand, some of the happiest efforts to create co-operative societies of production have been made in France. One of the most interesting of these establishments is that founded by M. Godin le Maire at Guise. He employs 900 workmen who call themselves the Familistère de Guise, and maintain among themselves the most intimate social relations. Their employer has exhibited an earnest solicitude to promote the welfare of his workmen. In 1859 he constructed for their accommodation, at a cost of 800,000 francs, a house, containing 250 separate tenements, which he lets to the workmen, at rents calculated to pay 3½ per cent. upon the capital expended. The value of this property has been divided into shares purchasable by the tenants, who may thus have an opportunity of becoming the sole proprietors. M. Godin le Maire has also divided the value of his plant and works into shares of the value of 25 francs each, by which means he aimed at associating the

CHAP. XIII.

whole body of his workmen with himself, as his partners in his business.

Co-operation in England. Experiment of Messrs. Briggs.

In England the effort to introduce the co-operative principle made by Messrs. Briggs remains still an experiment, though a hopeful experiment. The workmen are shareholders to a limited extent. Of 9,770 shares only 264 are held by the workmen, and Mr. Briggs is of opinion that, without more education, mining could not be conducted on a strictly co-operative system. In other branches of trade, co-operation appears to be making considerable progress. In Lancashire, as I noticed on the occasion of a recent visit, the improvement in the cotton trade has had the accustomed effect of encouraging the erection of new cotton mills; but at Middleton, the point of observation I happened to occupy, I was rejoiced to find that most of the new mills were established on the co-operative system.

Co-operative mills in Lancashire.

Co-operation in America.

In New York the Tailors' Association recently announced that their aim would be henceforth to throw over the system of strikes, and to commence fighting with the strongest weapon, Co-operation. Several Co-operative Land and Building Societies and Foundries have been established. An Iron Foundry was started in 1866 at Troy, in New York, with a capital of 2,750*l.* In the first year thirty-two men were employed, in 1869, eighty-five: the skilled men earning 35*l.* a year more than the wages paid in an ordinary foundry.

Co-operative wages the standard rate.

With these examples before us, we may venture to hope that co-operation may be more largely introduced into British industry. When this change has been brought about, the workmen will have a standard by which they can determine the fair rate of wages in their trade. They will know that they cannot expect from their employers a rate of pay exceeding that in the co-operative establishments, where the workmen themselves sit in judgment on the relative claims of capital and labour.

The Co-operative Association, working side by side with the capitalist, would diffuse among the workmen in the trade a knowledge of the state of affairs which

CHAP. XIII.

Co-operative experience would teach the anxieties of the capitalist.

would make such a mistake as that committed at Wigan impossible. Co-operation would teach our industrial population to appreciate the difficulties and hazards attending the investment of capital in business. I have had an opportunity of seeing what they are; and I can assure the working-man—whose stock in trade is secure amid all the fluctuations of commercial life, because it consists of his individual experience and dexterity, of which no reverse of fortune can deprive him—that the more precarious tenure by which capital is held, capital which has only been amassed after long years of thrift and untiring exertion, ought to mitigate the envy which the contemplation of the rare instances of great success in commercial enterprise may arouse. In the difficult vocation of a railway contractor the fluctuations and anxieties of business are felt with peculiar severity. I know of one great contract in which three partners together lost 750,000*l.* I could enumerate other contracts in which, though the actual loss was not so serious, the result was even more disastrous in proportion to the limited extent of the operations.

Lord Derby on co-opera-

The advantages of co-operation were summarised by Lord Derby in a well-considered and suggestive speech. "It is human nature," he said, "that a man should like to feel that he is to be the gainer by any extra industry that he may put forth, that he would like to have some sense of proprietorship in a shop or a mill, or whatever it may be, in which he knows his days; and it is because the system introduced of late years of co-operative industry meets that natural wish that I look forward to its extension with so much hopefulness. I believe it is the best and surest remedy for that antagonism of labour and capital which we hear so much talked of, and which to a certain extent no doubt exists." . . . . "I am well aware that such a state of things as I have pointed out, is one which cannot be brought about in a day. It is quite probable that there are some trades and some kinds of business in which it cannot be brought about at all; but it seems to me that it is in that direction that

CHAP. XIII.

the efforts of the best workers and the ideas of the best thinkers are tending; and we are not to be disheartened by a few failures, or disappointed because we do not at once hit upon the best way of doing what has never been done before." The diffusion of education under the recent Act will doubtless assist the industrial classes to overcome the difficulties of co-operative organization; and when a higher scale of education is given to the people than the purely elementary instruction which is now proposed, the great quality of self-help will be more highly developed.

CHAPTER XIV.

PIECE WORK.

Piece work and slave labour.

IT has been always the aim of experienced employers to give to the workman a direct interest in doing his work with skill and diligence. Slave labour, in which the motive of self-interest is wholly wanting, is on that very ground as unsatisfactory in an economical sense, as it is repugnant to our moral sentiments. Adam Smith truly says that "the person, who can acquire no property can have no other interest but to eat as much and labour as little as possible. In ancient Italy, how much the cultivation of corn degenerated, and how unprofitable it became to the master, when it fell under the management of slaves, is remarked both by Pliny and Columella." Slave labour was employed at

CHAP. XIV.

one time by my father's representative, Mr. Hancox, on the drainage works at Rio Janeiro; but he soon discovered that free Portuguese labour, even with wages at 4*s*. 6*d*. a day, was infinitely cheaper than the labour of the slaves.

Evidence before Committee on West Indian Colonies, 1847.

Some interesting evidence, as to the relative costs of free and slave labour, was given by witnesses who appeared before the Select Committee on the West Indian Colonies in 1847. It was stated by Mr. John Scoble, that free labour was not only the cheapest, but, under proper direction, the best kind of labour. The price of female slave labour, per month of twenty days, was ten dollars, or 1*s*. 9*d*. a day. The cost of rearing a slave up to the age of fourteen was 100*l*. In his opinion, if there had been a diminution in the production of sugar, there had on the other hand been a reduction in the cost of raising it.

Correspondence with Earl Grey in 1848.

In 1848 a correspondence took place between Earl Grey and the Governors of the sugar-growing colonies, relative to the causes of the then prevalent distress. Much evidence was given to prove that, at least in some of the colonies, the cost of production by free labour was less than the cost of doing the same work with slave labour.

Sir William Reid stated that the produce in Jamaica, under free labour cultivation, averaged one ton per acre; whereas in the most prosperous days, before the emancipation of the slaves, 18 cwts. per acre had been esteemed an excellent result.

The British Consul at Pernambuco gave a detailed statement of the comparative cost of work done by slaves, and work done by free labour. He stated that eighty slaves on an estate in Pernambuco, used to produce 171½ tons of sugar. The annual cost of maintaining the slaves, including replacement, was 765*l.* Adding to this sum interest at 12 per cent. on the first cost of the slaves, which he estimated at 4,050*l.* there was an additional expenditure of 486*l.* This gave the sum of 4,251*l.* as the total cost of producing the above quantity of sugar with slave labour.

The cost of producing an equal quantity of sugar by free labour was considerably less.

CHAP XIV.

The wages of the free labourer, without food, were $10\frac{3}{4}d.$ a day; free men were admitted to work harder than slaves; but, allowing that an equal number of free labourers should be employed, the total cost would have amounted only to 1,080*l.*

Piece work.

While I trust that the co-operative movement may be more successful in future than in the past, the difficulties which have been hitherto encountered may perhaps tend to reconcile those who have hitherto objected to piece work, to its adoption in default of a more perfect system.

Always adopted on railway contracts.

My father always preferred putting a price upon the work, rather than paying by the day. This system was modified to suit the usual habits of the people with whom he had to deal. The Piedmontese on the line from Chambery to Modane were paid at so much a barrow load. This minute measurement was exclusively the Piedmontese system. Piece work could not in all cases be adopted without some complications and difficulties; but my father always looked upon day work as a losing game; and all his work was done as far as possible by sub-contract, which is piece work on a somewhat larger scale. Even the scaffolding for the erection of an iron bridge, such as that over the Severn, near Colebrook Dale, of 200 feet span, was carried out upon the principle of sub-contract; and the same system was adopted for the excavation of shafts and adjacent lengths of tunnel. Payment by piece is beneficial alike to the master and the man. The men earn higher wages, while the master has the satisfaction of obtaining an equivalent for the wages he has paid, and completing the contract which he has undertaken with far greater rapidity. On public works the differences in the earnings of the men doing piece work, and men working by the day, were always remarkable. In the canal making days, men working in butty-gangs would earn 4*s*., while others working on the day work system would not earn more than from 2*s*. to 3*s*. a day.

There was a remarkable illustration of the advantage of piece work over day work in the construction of the railway between

CHAP. XIV.

Leicester and Hitchin. At the commencement of the works, instead of paying the workmen at so much per cubic yard, the piece work system was abandoned, and the men received the average amount of the agricultural wages of the country, namely, 2*s.* 3*d.* a day. On my father's attention being directed to this subject, the system was changed, and piece work introduced. It was found that when the men were paid by the day, the excavation in the cuttings had cost 1*s.* 6*d.* a yard. When the system was changed, day work abandoned, and piece work adopted, the cost of the work was reduced to 7*d.* per yard.

Objections to piece work.

Piece work is not popular with the English Trades Unions; and the objection urged by our own workmen is repeated by the artisans abroad. In a letter addressed by F. Fonché to M. Haussontier, published in the "Reports of Working Men on the Paris Exhibition," it is said that piece work, when executed on equitable terms, is a good thing in itself; but, the *marchandeur*, or small contractor, always wants to increase his profits by lessening the prices paid to the working people.

Objections have been raised to piece work by Mr. Thornton, in his essay on Labour, mainly on the ground that it makes men overtask themselves and contract intemperate habits, and tends to lower the remuneration of labour. On railways, however, it is certain that these objections have not been felt, and I could quote, in answer to Mr. Thornton, the opinions of Mr. Mill, Mr. McCulloch, and other economists, who have given their cordial approval to the system.

Workmen always work hard when paid by the piece.

I have no fear that the workman will not put forth his best skill and greatest energy, when encouraged to do so by the hope of reward. In my small personal experience I have seen much to confirm this opinion, expressed by Adam Smith, that "workmen when they are liberally paid by the piece, are very apt to overwork themselves, and ruin their constitution in a few years."

The truth of his position is in many cases incontrovertible. Perhaps one of the most striking cases is that of the slaves, employed as coffee carriers in the Brazils. These men are employed in removing bags of coffee, weighing from two to three hundredweight on their heads, in and out of large warehouses and from the warehouses to the shipping. They often carry these immense weights a distance of 300 or 400 yards. The men are the most powerful slaves in the Brazils, and they are paid at a fixed rate, in proportion to the amount of work performed. They work with the most intense vigour, in order to earn as soon as possible a sufficient sum, wherewith to purchase their freedom, and generally succeed in accumulating the amount required in three or four years. But they are a short-lived race, and in their devouring anxiety to accomplish their object, too often sacrifice their health by over exertion; although they are well fed on dried meat or salt meat from the river Plate, eaten with a large quantity of farinaceous food.

It would, in the present condition of trade, be simply impossible to entertain the notion of a further reduction of hours. But I hope to see the day when the progress of mechanical invention and habits of greater diligence on the part of workmen may enable them to earn as good a day's wages, and do as much work for their employer, in eight hours as in nine. In order, however, to accomplish so great a reform, the Trades Unions must no longer interpose, enforcing upon all workmen a regulated diligence, and preventing them from making the best use of their powers. I do not wish to see men overwork themselves. I believe with Adam Smith that "the man who works so moderately as to be able to work constantly, not only preserves his health the longest, but, in the course of the year, executes the greatest quantity of work." On the other hand, I have seen much listlessness and idleness in the workshop; and I look forward to the time when there may be more continued attention to business during the working hours, and when the workman shall receive a proportionate reward in shorter hours of labour.

CHAPTER XV.

COURTS OF CONCILIATION.

CHAP XV.

Courts of Conciliation.

IN times of commercial depression, the importance of establishing friendly means of adjusting the rival claims of capital and labour is underrated. When the rapid increase of production is checked, and especially when the rate of production is diminished, the competition among the industrial classes for employment makes it impossible for labour, however skilfully organized, to exact any concessions from capital. It often happens, in periods of unsuccessful trade, that mills are kept running, mines are being worked, and that engineering establishments are in operation, although the results may involve the employer in serious loss. In such cases production is continued, partly for the sake of sparing to the workmen the suffering arising from suspension of industry, partly also with the hope of a return of better trade. But it will be readily understood that under such adverse circumstances the employers cannot possibly entertain demands for an augmentation of wages. The case is reversed in periods of commercial prosperity, when an increasing production in all branches of industry affords employment to every individual who is able to work. The competition of unemployed labour is no longer felt, and labour will naturally begin to seek for an increased reward. The certainty that these claims will arise is a strong reason why some effort should be made to establish friendly and impartial tribunals by which they can be reviewed. Education will probably do much to develop the usefulness of courts of conciliation. It may be that a court of conciliation can never adjust a real quarrel. But it is certain that it may do much to prevent a quarrel from arising. If the workmen were satisfied that an employer could not make a concession without suffering serious loss, they would not

CHAP. XV.

be so unreasonable as to ask for it. The constant meeting of employers and representatives of the operatives at the same table must naturally facilitate peaceful negotiation where a desire for peace exists on both sides. With constant discussion coming events will cast their shadows before, and disputes are not likely suddenly to arise.

Courts of Conciliation established by Mr. Mundella after the model of the Conseils des Prud'hommes.

Much advantage might be expected from courts of arbitration, on the plan recommended by Mr. Mundella and Mr. Rupert Kettle. These courts of conciliation are an imitation of the Conseils des Prud'hommes in France. Each council was there established by decree of the government, and consisted of a president, a vice-president, not necessarily either employers or workmen, and six members elected by employers and workmen; the general aim is to obtain a settlement of trade disputes by judges who are the equals of the disputants. The proceedings are inexpensive; the judges are unpaid; and a delegation of the council, consisting of one employer and one workman, sit in judgment almost daily. The result, in ninety-five out of one hundred cases brought before these tribunals is a reconciliation between the parties ; and though appeals are permitted to the superior courts of law, they are rarely made.

Conseils des Prud'hommes approved by Lord Brougham.

The Conseils des Prud'hommes were highly approved by Lord Brougham who, in a debate in the House of Lords in 1859, on the strike in the building trade, referred to the efficiency with which the disputes between masters and men in France were adjusted. "It was impossible," he said, "to read the annual report of the proceedings of the Conseils des Prud'hommes, without wishing to see some analagous provisions in our own law;" and he stated that "in 1850, 28,000 disputes had been heard before the Conseils des Prud'hommes, of which no less than 26,800 were satisfactorily settled."

Employers should be more communicative.

It would be well if employers were to acquire the habit of giving more unreserved explanations as to the conditions and prospects of trade.

Switzerland.

It seems to me that in England we should do well to study the state of society in Switzerland, as described by Mr. Bonar. In

CHAP. XV.

Switzerland the personal relations between employers and employed are far more intimate and cordial than with us. Persons of every grade of society sit side by side in the cafés and places of amusement. The admission of workmen into the communal councils, where they share with their employers the responsibilities and honours of public life, while it encourages a wholesome spirit of independence, does much to establish a mutual feeling of sympathy and regard. Sometimes a want of cordiality in the demeanour of the employer is misinterpreted, as indicating a want of sympathy and kindness of heart. A little more facility of manner towards faithful and deserving workmen would often encourage sentiments of loyal good will, beneficial alike to the master and the man.

My father's friendly manner with workmen.

When I had the privilege of accompanying my lamented father on visits of inspection to works under construction, I was ever deeply impressed by his genial manner towards his old followers. He used to recognise many of the old navvies, even some whom he had not

CHAP. XV.

met for years, and address them by their Christian names. He would never omit to shake hands cordially with old gangers and sub-contractors, and when he met them on the works he would generally pull up for a few minutes, to talk over old times and ask after mutual acquaintances who had been employed on former contracts. A small manifestation of kindness like this, how little it costs; how much it is valued!

Conspicuous examples of harmony between employer and employed.

At the Exhibition in Paris in 1867 premiums were offered for conspicuous success in establishing friendly relations between masters and men. Many interesting examples of well-rewarded effort in this direction were produced from Germany. The case of M. Quiltolf, a manufacturer of Portland cement at Stettin, was among the most gratifying. When the war broke out in Austria, his affairs became seriously embarrassed. On hearing of the difficulties in which he was involved, his workmen were deeply concerned on his behalf. To avert his impending bankruptcy, they not only submitted to a reduction of 33 per cent. on their

M. Quiltolf.

CHAP. XV.

wages, but they lent him all their savings. M. Quiltolf had won for himself their grateful attachment by the paternal interest which he had always manifested towards them. They had lived together as one united family. Every Sunday in the summer M. Quiltolf had been in the habit of going out with his workmen, 500 in number, to an island at the mouth of the Oder, where they were accustomed to spend the afternoon in singing choral music.

Baron Diergard.

Many other examples of the same truly patriarchal relations between the employers and the employed, were brought under the notice of the Commissioners of the Exhibition at Paris in 1867. There was the case of the Baron Diergardt, a manufacturer of velvet, at Vierson, in Rhenish Prussia. When he celebrated the fiftieth anniversary of the formation of his establishment, many of his operatives celebrated the fiftieth anniversary of their entering his service. It would be easy to extend this enumeration, but it is impossible to give all the numerous examples, of which this may be taken as a type, which were produced from every country.

Benefi-cence of English employers.

Many of the largest English employers deserve the gratitude of the working classes for the considerate interest they have exhibited in their welfare, and the beneficence with which they have endeavoured to provide for their wants. In his report of October 1866, Mr. Redgrave speaks in terms of warm commendation of the institutions connected with Messrs. J. Akroyd and Sons at Halifax, which comprise every element for the assistance, morally, materially, and intellectually, of every person employed in the works.

Similar provision has been made by Messrs. J. Crossley and Sons at Halifax; by Messrs. Salt at Saltaire; and by many other benevolent employers.

Lamenta-ble separa-tion of classes.

It is melancholy to think how true it is that one-half the world knows not how the other half lives. In our great cities the tendency of the different classes to occupy separate quarters brings many social evils in its train—want of sympathy, indifference, it may be hostility, between poor and rich. I

CHAP. XV.

have often felt that it is much to be lamented that our successful employers of labour are apt to withdraw from the scene of their labours, and become country gentlemen, members of Parliament, or residents abroad. The love of field sports which makes country life so attractive, the patriotism which sends the man of business to the House of Commons, are doubtless admirable traits in the national character; but the withdrawal of the personal influence of the employer, just when it is becoming most valuable, is deeply to be regretted.

Prevalence of destitution.

Much has been accomplished in recent years to ameliorate the condition of the poor, but notwithstanding all the efforts which have been made, it is sad to think how large a proportion of our fellow countrymen are still far too familiar with the pressure of anxiety and want.

> . . . a thirst so keen
> Is ever urging on the vast machine
> Of sleepless labour, 'mid whose dizzy wheels
> The power least prized, is that which thinks and feels.

In the language of the Emperor Napoleon,

CHAP. XV.

Speech of Napoleon III.

in his speech to the Conseil d'États on March 13, 1869, "It must be acknowledged that the society in which we live contains many opposing elements. Do we not indeed see, on the one hand, legitimate aspirations and a just desire for improvement, and on the other subversive theories and criminal covetousness? The duty of the Government is to satisfy the former with resolution, and to reject the latter with firmness. If we fathom the diseases of the most flourishing people, we still discover, beneath an appearance of prosperity, many unmerited misfortunes calling for the sympathy of all generous hearts, many unsolved problems calling for the united action of all reflecting minds."

As we think on these things, we may sometimes be prone to despair of the perfectibility of human institutions, and to fold our arms and idly wait the fulfilment of our inexorable destiny.

Encouragement for the future in the past.

But if we are sometimes inclined to despair, we shall find encouragement to go forward in a bolder spirit by the contemplation of the victories already won. The story has

CHAP. XV.

been compendiously recorded in the work of Messrs. Ludlow and Lloyd Jones, on the progress of the working classes. Subsequently to 1833 the Factories Acts, the Ten Hours Act, the Mines and Collieries Acts, the Acts relating to Merchant Seamen; the establishment of Loan Societies, the Post Office Savings' Banks, the Friendly and Benefit Building Societies, the creation of a National System of Education, the Penny Postage, the adoption of a new and more liberal fiscal policy, the facilities given for establishing public libraries and museums, the remission of the paper duties and the creation of a cheap press, the enlargement of the franchise, which has given to the working classes an overwhelming share of political power, and last, and perhaps the greatest of these reforms, the extension of educational facilities to every child, testify to the generous spirit of our recent legislation in all that relates to the welfare of the industrial classes.

Social improvement not the work of the legislature.

The importance of social reforms, and of securing the material well-being of the masses of our population, is now universally recognised. I confess my doubts as to the efficacy of legislation in such matters. It must be remembered that all national expenditure for the benefit of the working classes which is not reproductive, must be defrayed by additional taxes. Let the transfer of land be by all means facilitated, let railway communication between the centre of a great city and its suburbs be made as cheap as possible, let emigration be assisted by loans, if security can be taken for the repayment of such advances; but, granted that something may be done by these various means, I hesitate to admit that the State can be the chief instrument for elevating still higher the moral condition of the people. The work is too vast for any Government to undertake. It can only be accomplished by the self-help and self-sacrifice of the whole nation. And when all shall have done their duty in their several stations, the pressure of unforeseen calamity upon some unhappy individuals and the incapacity of others will leave a mass of suffering to our compassionate care, which it will tax our best energies to relieve. The poor we shall always have with us; and the great peers, the landowners, and the men who have become rich in commerce, must show themselves active in their sympathies for all just demands, benevolent and kindly in the presence of distress. The exercise of these excellent virtues, while it is in the first place a paramount duty, will undoubtedly bring with it to the State and the society in which we live, the immediate and priceless blessing of social union and contentment.

The condition of civilised man will be raised, not by destroying all the institutions which we have inherited from the wisdom of past ages, but by earnestly applying ourselves to adapt that which exists, and the value of which has been tested by time and by experience to the ever new requirements of mankind.

In the eloquent language of Mr. Ruskin, "If we labour faithfully we shall know that in reverence is the chief joy and power of life—reverence for what is pure and bright in our own youth, for what is true and tried in the age of others, for all that is gracious among the living, great among the dead, and marvellous in the powers that cannot die."

The quality of self-help will be developed best in those peoples who are most ready to appreciate the obligations and the practical lessons of Christianity. "In societies such as ours," says M. Michel Chevalier, "in which the inequality of fortune presents a striking contrast beside our political equality, the religious sentiment is the best means of reconciling and uniting together the rich and the poor. It teaches the rich man to have a due regard for his disinherited brother. It teaches the poor man to be patient and honest amid all temptations, to be confident of a brighter future here below, which can only be attained by his own intelligent exertion, and to look beyond the world to the hope of a good reward in another and higher sphere of existence." The vague theory of the International Society, founded on atheism and in a narrow and contemptible spirit, acknowledging the existence of only one section of society, will never gain a footing among us, if only those whose responsi-

CHAP. XV.

bilities are great will manfully endeavour to do their duty. It is because there has been so much public spirit among us that we have hitherto been preserved from the miseries of civil war, and the continued development of these public virtues is our best security for the future.

INDEX

LONDON: PRINTED BY
SPOTTISWOODE AND CO., NEW-STREET SQUARE
AND PARLIAMENT STREET

www.ingramcontent.com/pod-product-compliance
Lightning Source LLC
LaVergne TN
LVHW020241110826
845151LV00003B/996

* 9 7 8 1 4 2 5 5 3 0 5 5 6 *